JAMES MAY
OH COOK!

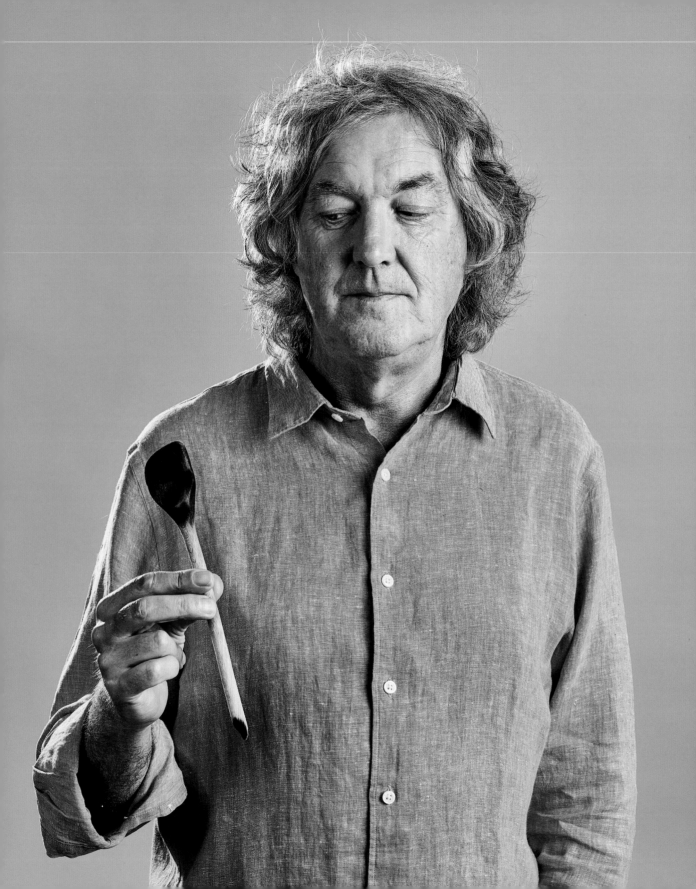

JAMES MAY
OH COOK!

60 EASY RECIPES THAT ANY IDIOT CAN MAKE

PAVILION

DEDICATION

To Gordon Ramsay, with best wishes for his imminent retirement.

First published in the UK in 2020 by
Pavilion Books Company Limited
43 Great Ormond Street, London WC1N 3HZ

www.pavilionbooks.com

ISBN 978-1-91166-315-7

A CIP catalogue record for this book is available from the British Library.

10 9 8 7 6

Publisher: Helen Lewis
Managing editor: Fiona Holman
Editor: Cara Armstrong
Illustrations on page 14 by Kang Kuo Chen
TV stills: Will Fisher
Photography: Martin Poole
Food stylist: Rosie Reynolds
Prop stylist: Lydia McPherson
Design: Smith & Gilmour

Reproduction by Rival Colour Ltd, UK
Printed in the UK by CPI Colour

CONTENTS

A WORD FROM ME

Hello readers. I may be wasting my time writing this introduction. As I sit here, with my plate of Fortnum & Mason petits fours*, I have no idea what the contents of this book will be.

This is no ordinary cookery book. This is different, because the author can't cook. Usually, with these TV/cook-book tie-in jobs, the book comes first, and then selected bits are filmed for the show. The idea behind *Oh Cook!* is to learn on screen and then put the successful bits into print.

But, contrary to typical book-writing practice, I'm writing the introduction first, rather than after reviewing the finished work. Nothing has actually been cooked yet, and no recipes written up. So it could be that you'll never read this; that the whole endeavour will be remembered as nothing more than a mushroom cloud of oily smoke hanging briefly over Hammersmith before being plucked away by the wind, hopefully towards Chiswick.

I'll keep going anyway.

I shouldn't really be writing a cookery book or fronting a cooking TV show. My relationship with foodieism is a bit like the one the Archbishop of Canterbury has with Satan; that is, I renounce it.

The first thing that annoys me about all this is people who say, 'Oh, I love food,' as if it's somehow beyond the rest of us. I've never met anybody who doesn't like food. Everybody loves food. Ask some people who don't have any for confirmation of this.

It also bothers me that foodies embrace mass production, capitalism and globalisation in every other facet of their lives, but when it comes to food, they want it produced by bucolic peasants in smocks and sold at a 'market'. They wouldn't have an artisan smartphone or a craft pacemaker, but they want sausages produced by a man who husbanded his own pig or beer brewed according to a tradition that stretches all the way back to a marketing executive's lunch.

We should remember that the industrialisation of food production fed us and liberated us from the misery of lard and tripe, and while it's

*Not really. It's a packet of chocolate digestives.

fashionable to dismiss this, we must remember that to do so is a privilege born of canned soup and the frozen pizza.

I could go on, so I will. Many of the car programmes I've presented have been criticised because we drive around in Ferraris and Lamborghinis, and nobody does that in the real world. But are cooking shows and recipe books any different? Millions have enjoyed Gordon Ramsay's swearing and Nigella Lawson's heaving breasts, but most of us eat supermarket ready meals, just as most of us drive mid-sized diesel hatchbacks. It's largely fantasy, and the energy density of the world's unread cookery books would provide a year's electricity to a minor town, if it was acceptable to burn books.**

All this does worry me. We live in an age where too many restaurants serve buggered-about ingredients to bored people who really ought to find something creative or constructive to do; where the chef has become 'chef' and must be revered as a temperamental artist. Cooking is not art, it's a task.

Still; it's a task those of us who can't really cook may as well embrace. Everyone has to eat (the much-vaunted astronaut's meal pill of my childhood never materialised) and everyone has a kitchen of some sort (but see 'Essential Kit' on page 12 for an exception). Cooking is also much more accessible than driving supercars or collecting Renaissance art. It can be done for a few quid, using a handful of implements, and literally billions of people can do it, so it can't be that hard.

That's what this book is really about. Not a random assortment of recipes, which is like being given a fish, but a thought-out selection of recipes covering a range of basic techniques and principles, which is more like being taught to fish, if you remember that excruciating 1980s motivational poster. Jus, drizzles, foams, 'smashed' avocado, and 'a bed of' can come later. As Picasso said, you have to learn the rules like a pro if you are to break them like an artist.

Incidentally – if you're not reading this, it's because I thought 'sod it' and ordered a Deliveroo Chinese.

James

**It isn't. If you start burning books, Heinrich Heine told us, you end up burning people. He might have added 'and the cheese sauce'.

A NOTE ON INGREDIENTS

One of the things that annoys me about cookery books is the constant haranguing in the list of ingredients about using fresh this and that: fresh eggs, freshly squeezed lime juice, and the one that appears in every single list and makes me want to kick a cafetière to smithereens, freshly ground black pepper.

I'm not going to do that. Here's the deal. Use fresh, free-range and sustainable ingredients if you can, because it's definitely better. But if you can't, you don't have to give up and ring for a pizza. You can use packet and frozen stuff instead. You can even use ready grated Parmesan cheese if you don't have a conveniently buried wheel of it, as Samuel Pepys did. And if you can't draw milk straight from the churns of the merry maid mentioned in Tennyson's juvenilia, well, it's OK if you just buy some from the corner shop.

On the question of fresh or dried pasta, fresh pasta is not necessarily better than dried. It is just different. Many Italian cooks choose dried pasta over fresh and the best dried pasta still comes from Italy. I think dried pasta is easier for beginner cooks, as we are here.

We are learning to cook, and people learning portraiture use school poster paints, not expensive oils and pigments. Once we've learned the basics, we can hit the farmers' markets and wholefood supermarkets and become proper bores. But until then, we're just cooks.

A NOTE ON WEIGHTS AND MEASURES

Cooking is not engineering. The volume of milk in a cheese sauce is not critical in the way that the diameter of a piston is, or the mass of a blade in a jet engine, not least because tiny variations in that are compounded by the huge rotational speeds found in gas turbines.

I have to put a measure of some sort in the ingredients list, but it can be considered a guide at this stage in your development. As long as you're reasonably close, you'll be OK.

Apart from anything else, a lot of things will come at weights you can't control. I might call for a 200g/7oz steak, but the one you end up buying might be 230g/8oz. You're not going to cut a bit off to make the weight right. All eggs are different, not all salt is equally salty and the tomato is not mensurally defined under the SI system.

Units are another issue. I'm happy with metric, but imperial equivalents are also included because Americans seem to prefer them. Actually, I'm happy with both, in the same way that I can understand the price of things in pounds and dollars. They're only units.

Americans also like cups, whatever they are. We also have ounces, a unit of weight, and fluid ounces, which are a unit of volume. A tsp is a teaspoon and a tbsp is a tablespoon, but there's no international agreement on how big they are. It doesn't matter – they're approximate.

Elsewhere, I suggest 'handfuls' of an ingredient, such as parsley, to garnish. I mean as in enough to sprinkle on the top of whatever you're making. You know how much that is by looking. You're not going to weigh it out. A knob of butter, as I've been saying for years, is the size of a piece of cheese, and you already know how big that is.

A spot of oil in the middle of a frying pan is clearly not enough to cook an egg. It's obvious. If your chopped onions become completely submerged in melted butter, you used too much. You'll work it all out very quickly. All you need is 15g/½oz of common sense.

A NOTE ON TIMINGS

All cookery books will give you a preparation time and a cooking time for each recipe. The cooking time, providing you set the controls correctly, are a matter of record; time and temperature cannot be thwarted. But the preparation times are simply NEVER TRUE, and they're not true here.

If you're a seasoned cook (geddit?) or a professional, and your arms are a blur, then 15 minutes to prep a spag bol might be about right. But if you're a seasoned cook or a professional, you won't be reading this book. You are a beginner, and everything will take much longer.

The preparation times in this book can be considered a target, a bit like the lap record at a race circuit. Something to aim for, but you won't do it. You won't be able to do several complex bits at the same time, and after each stage you'll keep consulting the instructions. You'll stare at the ingredients meaningfully and possibly have a lie down or a beer while you think it through.

I'd double or even triple everything, based on my lengthy experience of not being able to cook. I once tried to make a chicken tikka bhuna from scratch, starting at an Indian supermarket buying raw spices that I then roasted and ground before making my own pastes and powders. The results were quite good but it took two days.

You might want to consider this when you're sending out the invitations.

ESSENTIAL KIT

Back in my student days, I was a vocal advocate of the minimalist kitchen. All you needed was a small knife, a big knife, a small pan, a big pan, a frying pan, a plate, a bowl, a knife, fork and a spoon. There was a communal chip pan as well, at least until someone set it on fire, and then it went out of the window. It's a shame no-one opened it first.

It helped that my canon of works was as streamlined as my equipment. Aside from the usual 'on toast' *oeuvre*, here is a list of things I could make:

Grilled pork chop with boiled potatoes and peas.

Bread came pre-sliced, cheese came pre-grated, gravy came as a type of dust, and our ambitions never strayed beyond immediate post-Victorian northern British workhouse fayre. No avocado, then, and a number of words that now form part of the everyday lexicon of eating hadn't yet been invented: organic, wholemeal, multi-grain, fresh. Why would you need a fish poacher? Or a spatula, even?

Around 15 years later I applied the same certainty of mind to the kitchen itself. Within a year of moving in to my first proper house, I'd returned home late from the pub with my mate Stanley and decided that the knotted pine country kitchen I'd inherited really wasn't very me, and that it should go. By 3am it had indeed gone: the fitted cupboards, the ergonomically sited double oven, the spindled shelving, the hand-made tiles with English flowers in relief; it was all outside in a pile, and I was left with a rude standpipe protruding from one wall (controlled by the master stop-cock) and a single-ring camping stove. But I survived, and guests were still able to enjoy pan-fried pork and onion with pulses in a tomato-based reduction.*

These days, I'm different. As a fully formed and middle-aged metrosexual (whatever that is. Apparently I am) I cannot walk past a kitchen shop without veering off to see what devices have been produced to address problems that my student kit wasn't asking.

At some point in my late 40s I realised that the kitchen is a workshop, where tools and materials come together to make things, and suddenly the whole business became very appealing. Heart-stoppingly expensive Japanese knives, shredders and stoners, synthetic chopping boards in bright colours, ricers, rice cookers, processors, whisks, waterstones for

*Spam and beans.

sharpening, woks, wasabi graters, garlic crushers, apple corers... the ambitions of those with all the gear but no idea are inexhaustible. These things cry out to me like abandoned kittens and I must have them. And I do.

But what, as a beginner, do you really need? I refer you to paragraph one. You'll be amazed at what you can do with that, and during my travels in places such as south-east Asia I've been amazed at what people crouching on the backs of barges could create with one utensil and one implement. Nevertheless, during the production of the Oh Cook! TV show I compiled a list. Here it is.

ESSENTIALS

Three saucepans – small, medium and large
Buy nice ones with decent thick bottoms, because they will last your whole life. I'm still using the ones I bought in 1991. Not that they've had that much use.

Cast iron casserole
You can use it on the cooker or in it. Cast iron will retain heat. Unbreakable and once used a bit, it will have the air of an archaeological find about it.

Vegetable steamer
You can boil veg in one of the pans above, but a steamer genuinely does a better job. Also, there is no nicer noise than a freshly prepared sprout bouncing off the thin stainless steel of a steamer.

Frying pan
A decently deep one, again with a thick bottom. Buy one with a lid, because the lid can be used when poaching. Non-stick is good but I don't think it's essential.

Oven dishes
Ceramic ones, in a few sizes, plus some enamel tin ones of a sort that would have been used by Dad's Army. You can make the likes of fish pie and lasagne in the ceramic ones, and a pastry-cased pie in the enamel ones.

Baking sheet
There was probably one that came with your oven.

Roasting pan
Not the same as a baking sheet, as it's much deeper. Don't be fooled by the disposable aluminium ones that appear in the run-up to Christmas. You'll want to use it again, at other times of the year.

Carving tray
If that's what it's called. I mean the stainless steel type with feet at one end to tilt it, and a well at the other to collect juices, and spikes in the middle to hold your chicken, joint or swan steady as you carve. You don't roast on this, it's where meat rests and juices run out to make gravy. [Ed: Do you really have one of these? JM: Oh yes. I thought everyone did.]

Chef's knives
Don't go mad, yet. You can buy sets of three for very little money, and they can be sharpened effectively if you know what you're doing. Buy a carving knife and fork as well. You know you want to.

Sharpening steel
A steel is still much better than any device that claims to make sharpening 'easy'. You'll have to learn to use it, but the satisfaction of brandishing knife and steel in a flourish of honing will be worth it.

Vegetable peeler
I have many, but my favourite is still the pivoting steel slotted type. A good one takes transparently thin shavings and reaches into the nooks and crannies of comedically shaped potatoes.

Chopping boards
Wood is preferred by many, and it's kind to knives, but I worry about hygiene. I would never cut meat on a wooden board. Buy a wooden one because it looks nice, and use it for vegetables and bread, and then buy a self-healing plastic one for meat and fish. They can be boiled or shoved in the dishwasher.

Wooden spoon
There's not much excuse for using wood in the modern world, but wooden spoons turn into fascinating heirlooms. My best one is 30 years old.

Spatulas

Heatproof plastic ones are ace, and won't damage non-stick pans. As thin as possible is best. Also buy a stainless one for extra thinness, and because it can be used as a rudimentary musical instrument. See Gazunder opposite.

Slotted spoon, serving spoon and ladle

Explanation unnecessary.

Potato masher

The plastic ones with a bevelled edge are surprisingly good.

Whisk

You don't need a mechanical one. Just a balloon-shaped thing. Not too big or it won't go into corners.

Box grater

With different shapes on each face. Will do everything, including your fingers.

Colander and sieve

The former in steel or aluminium with large holes (mine is at least 70 years old); the latter in plastic with a mesh. You can also use the sieve to make a rudimentary steamer for veg.

Can opener

Duh.

Grabbers

Tongs of some sort. Elliptical, square, flat, bowled; doesn't matter, as long as they grab.

Corkscrew and bottle opener

The most important tool you'll buy, as all cooking begins with opening a bottle of something. Even if you decide on a takeaway, you'll need to open the wine or beer. Use a 'waiter's friend' type. Reject fancy corkscrews in presentation boxes.

NICE TO HAVE

Ruinously expensive knives

from Japan, Sweden, Germany and elsewhere. The knife is the most important tool, as most things in cooking start off too big – cows, pumpkins, cinnamon trees, etc. Really good knives are a joy to use and an acceptable outlet for fetishism. Much of the May household's kitchen equipment is old, battered, and in some cases, rather like fine paintings, acquired by descent. But my personal collection of a dozen or so knives belongs to me, and me alone, and were all selected by me, and no-one else is allowed to touch them.

Waterstone [Ed: Do you mean a whetstone? JM: No, waterstone. Whetstones are loaded with oil, waterstones are soaked in water. Much nicer and cleaner to use.]

Honing on a waterstone is a true craft skill, but once you've managed it, you'll be able to produce knives of surgical lethality and amaze your friends.

Large meat cleaver

Useless in the kitchen unless you're doing your own butchery, but great for scaring off annoying trick-or-treat kids at Halloween. Garnish along the edge with tomato purée.

Food processor

Can kick the crap out of stubborn foodstuffs in a few seconds. These jobs take hours by hand.

Rice cooker

They work. You can do it in a pan but it takes management. The rice cooker is a load-and-forget culinary weapon. You won't regret it.

Pestle and mortar

You will begin by buying spices in powdered form, but eventually you will want to try grinding them up yourself. This is how. Not been bettered since ancient Egypt.

Mouli rotary grater

The greatest single invention in the kitchen. Saves your fingers, and delivers bonus cheese pieces to the cook. Infinitely restorable.

Gazunder

A thing a bit like a large glazier's putty knife and very thin. So called because it 'goes under' things, like slices of cake and pizza. See Spatulas opposite.

Wok

A wok hanging on the wall or left lying around ostentatiously is a signifier of great sophistication, or so we believe. If you're going to have one, have a proper steel one, the thinner the better. The thick non-stick ones will be despised by your Asian guests. Steel ones take more management, because you have to oil them after use to stop them rusting. But they eventually turn almost black on the inside and become artworks of a sort.

NOT NECESSARY, BUT...

Phwoar! Absolutely everything else in the kitchen shop.

A NOTE ON GADGETS

Some kitchen gadgets can be categorised, like Velcro, under 'What did we do before…', but others belong in the bin. Here is some ruthless consumer advice on those we tried during the filming of *Oh Cook!*

RUBBER EGG POACHER
PAGE 23

VEGETABLE DICER
PAGE 26

CHOPPER UPPERER
PAGE 37

WHEELIE HERB CHOPPER
PAGE 54

MULTI SCISSORS
PAGE 60

SHEEP-SHAPED FLOUR HOOVER
PAGE 86

VOMITING CHICKEN
PAGE 119

A NOTE ON OVEN DISHES

My kitchen cupboard of kit contains around a dozen oven dishes of some description, ceramic, earthenware and enamelled, each one of them a different size yet none of them the size I actually want.

There is some sort of culinary law of sod going on here. You could own every oven dish made since one first appeared in a cave painting, but you would still want one a bit bigger. Or smaller.

Which one do you use? Here's a good tip for beginners. Let's say you're going to make a shepherd's pie. This will almost certainly start with a supermarket pack of minced lamb. You need a dish a bit bigger all round than the pack, because that will leave space for the other ingredients and the potato topping. Not smaller.

Now you can judge how many potatoes you will need for the topping. Put a few potatoes in the selected oven dish. Will they cover it to a uniform depth of 2cm/¾ inch when mashed up? That's the right amount.

This is a bit harder with something like a lasagne, but if you imagine each layer to be around a finger's width deep, you can work it out. Select the planform dimensions of the lasagne dish based on the pasta sheets. Minimise trimming. Never use a circular dish for lasagne. The pasta is rectangular.

As a good general rule, anything encased in pastry should be baked in a metal dish, as they transfer heat better. Everything else can be baked in any old dish. But not Tupperware.

CHAPTER ONE
BRUNCH

BOILED EGG
WITH AVO AND PROSCIUTTO 'SOLDIERS'

This simple recipe is offered as a riposte to the fashion for serving avocado 'smashed'. Here the avocado is spared this indignity, and served instead as a solid dipping instrument. Bear in mind the requirement for a 'just ripe' avocado. Nothing will disguise an under-ripe one and an over-ripe one will turn to smash.

SERVES 2
PREP TIME: 10 MINUTES
COOKING TIME: 13 MINUTES

1 just ripe avocado
4 slices of prosciutto,
    halved lengthways
2 big eggs, at room
    temperature

Are my eggs fresh?
Drop (carefully) an egg into a bowl of cold water. If it sinks, then, like a witch, it's good. If it floats, there has been bacterial activity within and it's bad. Discard, or use as a challenging air-rifle target.

Storing eggs
Eggs can go in the fridge, and stored thus are good for two weeks or more (see above). For some reason, professionals like to store them pointy end down. As egg shells are porous, keeping them in the box saves them from being corrupted by all the leftover curry also in there. Remove eggs from the fridge at least 30 minutes before using, especially if boiling them. They will break in the hot water otherwise.

Preheat the oven to 200ºC/400ºF.

Halve the avocado and remove the stone carefully. You can do this by hammering the point of a knife into it with the back of a spoon, and then giving it a sharp twist.

Divide each avocado half into four, lengthways. These pieces have to be thin enough to just fit into the boiled egg.

Remove the skin from each piece. You will probably be able to lift it off with a fingernail. Otherwise, use a large, shallow spoon to scoop the flesh away from the skin.

Wrap the slices of prosciutto around the full length of the avo pieces, in a spiral, and place them on a baking sheet lined with baking parchment.

Bake for around 10 minutes, or until the prosciutto turns crispy. Drain on kitchen roll while you boil the eggs.

For perfect dipping eggs, bring a medium pan of water to the boil and keep it 'rolling'; that is, bubbling vigorously and making a noise.

Gently lower the eggs into the water with a slotted spoon. If the eggs are taken straight from the fridge, they may crack during boiling and develop strange white beards.

Boil for 4-5 minutes.

Remove the eggs from the pan and place each one in an egg cup. Smash the egg's head in and start dipping.

Unusually, it's the camera that's out of focus ↓

CLASSIC OMELETTE

*Here is the technique for an absolutely bog-standard egg-only omelette.
Once you've got it right, and it's lightly browned on the outside but runny and
hot in the middle, you can start experimenting with adding all those extra bits
found at the 'omelette station' in a slightly tragic business hotel: cheese,
ham, onion, peppers, chillies, mushrooms, Spam.*

SERVES 1
PREP TIME: 5 MINUTES
COOKING TIME: 5 MINUTES

2 medium eggs
1 tbsp milk
A medium knob of
    unsalted butter
Salt 'n' pepper

Break the eggs into a bowl. Mix them up with a wooden spoon but without whisking them, or you'll get scrambled eggs.

Season with salt and pepper and stir in the milk.

Heat the butter in a non-stick frying pan until it is foaming gently but not turning brown.

Pour in the egg mixture, stirring cautiously with the wooden spoon, and drawing the mixture in from the edges for a neatly defined circle of sorts. (If you're adding extras, now is the time to toss them in.)

Once the bottom half of the eggy puddle has set, stop stirring and allow it to cook for around half a minute.

Now, with a long, thin spatula, fold one half of the circle over the other.

Slide onto a warmed plate. It should be just turning brown on the pan side but still yellow on the inside.

Have another go.

KEDGEREE

Kedgeree is a king of breakfasts, supposedly a British thing but one that came down to us from the Mughal rulers of India. Some people would have you use milk instead of water for poaching the fish and for cooking the rice, but I think that makes it too smooth. I like the feral quality of this version. Choose pale undyed smoked haddock if possible. This will feed two fatties. To divide among four, make two extra poachies.

SERVES 2 FATTIES
PREP TIME: 15 MINUTES
COOKING TIME: 30 MINUTES

300g/10½oz chunky
    pale undyed smoked
    haddock fillet, skin on
50g/1¾oz/¼ cup butter
1 small onion, peeled
    and diced
1 tsp medium curry powder,
    or Madras if you're
    feeling bold
110g/3½oz/½ cup
    basmati rice
A large handful of flat
    leaf parsley, chopped
1 tbsp lemon juice
2 really fresh big eggs
A drop or 2 of white wine
    vinegar (more of this in
    the panel opposite)
Salt 'n' pepper

Place the haddock fillet in a large frying pan (choose one with a lid) and cover with cold water. Bring this to the boil, then add the lid, lower the heat and simmer for about 6–8 minutes.

It's important not to overcook the fish, or it will become rubbery. Poke a knife between the flakes and see if the flesh has turned almost opaque. 'Tis done.

Transfer the fish onto a plate using a wide guzunder or two spatulas, and keep the poaching water, as you will need it later. Pour it into a measuring jug. Cover the fish and place in a warm oven.

Clean the frying pan and return it to the heat. Melt half of the butter and gently fry the onion until soft – about 5 minutes. Add the curry powder and cook for a minute or so before adding the rice and 225ml/8fl oz of the reserved poaching liquid, giving it a stir.

Once it is simmering, cover with the lid and cook very gently for about 10 minutes or until the rice is just tender. While this is happening, remove the fish from the oven, discard the skin and any bones from the fillet and break into large flakes.

Meanwhile, put a large pan of water onto the heat for the poached eggs.

Remove the frying pan from the heat, add the fish, parsley, lemon juice and remaining butter to the rice and fork through, season to taste and mix it up properly but without mangling it. Cover the pan with a folded tea towel and put it on a very, very low heat while you...

...poach the eggs.

Your large pan of water should now be boiling. Add a drop or two of white wine vinegar (this helps the egg white to solidify).

Crack an egg into a teacup or onto a saucer first. It allows you to check for shell debris and to see if the yolk is broken, in which case it's not your one. It will also be easier to tip the egg into the pan this way.

Stir the water in the pan to create a little whirlpool and gently slide the egg into the middle – this helps wrap the white around the yolk.

Turn down the heat to a simmer and cook for 4–5 minutes until the white is set, then remove from the water with a slotted spoon and drain on some kitchen roll. Repeat with t'other egg.

Divide the kedgeree between two warmed bowls and top each with an egg and serve.

Ruin the moment with a massive argument about how to poach an egg correctly (see below).

THE GREAT EGG POACHING DEBATE

The great taboos of British mealtime conversation are sex, religion and politics. But I don't quite buy this. I can have a proper row with one of my best mates about globalisation but we'll still be best mates the next day. Introduce the debate about how to poach eggs, and we may never speak to each other again.

Everyone knows exactly how to poach an egg and will brook no dissent. I certainly do. I use an egg-poaching pan. This is one of those pans with a holed insert and little plastic cups that sit in the boiling water underneath. There's a glass lid, so you can watch the action. Putting the lid on also cooks the tops of the eggs as steam is redirected towards them. Lid management is key to good, evenly poached eggs.

I like eggs poached this way because they remind me of my youth and are a comedic shape.

Strictly speaking, since you're about to tell me anyway, this pan is a coddler, not a poacher. Real egg poaching takes place directly in the water.

But I still think that the method of dropping a cracked directly into a pan of boiling water for a few minutes makes for a watery result. There are always snotty bits around the edge. If you drop the egg into still water it will come out flat as a pancake rather than as a well-shaped egg. Hence the belief that you should create a whirlpool with a spoon or balloon whisk (easier) before dropping in the egg. But I think the physics of this are suspect.

We are supposed to add a drop of white wine vinegar to the water to help the white of the egg bind – but not brown chip-shop malt vinegar, because that will definitely make the eggs taste vinegary. So now they're watery, snotty and vinegary, and they won't stay on the toast. My poacher makes bogie-free, emoji-style eggs that stay put.

This is only the beginning of the debate. Do you salt the water? Do you turn the heat off and put a lid on? Some even advocate cracking the egg into a small saucer or ramekin dish lined with lightly greased clingfilm before dropping it in the pan, but this might be one of those things like a weeping statue of the Madonna. No-one's actually seen it happen.

This drearily long argument can now be brought to a close, because the best way to poach an egg is by using the rubber thingy (see above). It really does work and there, as Dr Johnson would have said, is an end on 't.

We can now, as a species, move on. Probably to cheese sauce. Mustard or no?

SHAKSHUKA

This is especially popular in Israel, although everybody in the Middle East claims it as their own. It is in essence a vegetarian spicy tomato pizza without the base and with some eggs thrown in. 'Shakshuka', by the way, means 'all mixed up'. That's a clue. It makes a great sharing dish as it's quite tricky to remove from the pan in a meaningful way.

SERVES 4
PREP TIME: 15 MINUTES
COOKING TIME: 30 MINUTES

1 tbsp olive oil
1 medium onion,
    peeled and diced
1 red (bell) pepper,
    deseeded and diced
2 tsp smoked paprika
1 tsp ground cumin
½ tsp chilli powder
    (or more if feeling cocky)
2 garlic cloves, peeled
    and finely chopped
1 x 400g/14oz can of
    whole peeled tomatoes
4 big eggs
A small handful of coriander
    (cilantro) leaves, chopped
Salt 'n' pepper

In a deep frying pan, heat the oil and sweat the onion and pepper for around 5 minutes, or until the onion is translucent. Add the spices and garlic and cook for a couple more minutes.

Now add the tomatoes and salt and pepper to taste. Squash them down in the pan and mix them well with the other bits. Simmer gently for 15 minutes.

Now, with a large spoon, make four hollows at the points of the compass in the mixture. Crack an egg into each one. Cover the pan (ideally with the lid) and cook for 5–8 minutes, depending on how runny you want the eggs. They are poaching in the juice, and lid-on, lid-off management is key to cooking the bottoms and tops of the eggs equally.

Finish with a scattering of chopped coriander leaves. Serve with toast fingers for dipping, or flatbread. Eat your shakshuka straight out of the pan.

BLACK PUDDING HASH
WITH FRIED EGG

This is a pretty simple, one-pan fry-up. You could use Spam instead of black pudding if you prefer. For a vegetarian version use vegan black pudding (sic) which is made with compressed beetroot and is very tasty. Other vegetarian options include aubergine or mushrooms.

SERVES 4
PREP TIME: 10 MINUTES
COOKING TIME: 20 MINUTES

400g/14oz potatoes,
   diced into small cubes
   (this is a great opportunity
   to use the vegetable dicer)
   – robust floury potatoes
   are better than namby-
   pamby new ones, but
   any sort will do
2 tbsp vegetable oil,
   plus extra for the eggs
1 medium onion, peeled
   and finely chopped
1 red chilli, finely chopped
   (optional, but why not?)
200g/7oz black pudding,
   coarsely chopped in a
   rough and ready fashion
4 big eggs
A handful of flat leaf
   parsley, chopped
Salt 'n' pepper

Blanch the potatoes in boiling salted water for around 4 minutes, then drain well.

Heat the oil in a non-stick frying pan, add the potatoes and fry until they start to turn brown (after around 5 minutes). Add the onion and chilli, if using, stir and cook until soft. Season generously with salt 'n' pepper.

Add the black pudding. Mix it all up and fry for 5 minutes until the black pudding starts to become crispy.

While this is happening, fry your eggs. You could also poach them (see page 23), but why corrupt the entirely fried nature of this healthy breakfast item?

Mix the parsley through the hash, dollop it between 4 warmed plates and serve, topped with an egg.

A PERFECT FRIED EGG

In a small non-stick frying pan add more oil than you imagine is healthy and heat until the oil is beginning to smoke slightly. You can use butter, but it won't get as hot as oil and there's a risk of burning it.

Crack your egg into a teacup or small glass and pour the egg gently into the middle of the hot pan. It should crackle and spit. If not, the heat was too low. Using a spatula, push any errant white towards the centre.

For a sunny side up egg, use the spatula to flip a little hot oil onto the top of the yolk. It should go slightly cloudy. Or, put a lid on the pan for around a minute, to direct heat to the top of the egg.

For an easy-over egg, wait until the bulk of the white has solidified. Now take the pan in one hand, tilt it towards the other, then deftly slide your (thin) spatula underneath the egg and rotate the wrist while lifting slightly to turn it over. This action should take 1 second.

The perfect finished egg should have a firm white, a soft yolk and be starting to crisp up around the edges. Remove the egg from the pan and keep warm while you fry more.

VEGETABLE DICER

How it works Veg is placed on the square grid of sharp blades. Lid is then depressed, chips fall into tray below.

For Been popular for decades, because it works.

Against May remind you of being in the 1970s.

Destination Kitchen drawer of crap.

AMERICAN PANCAKES

This recipe makes 12 pancakes. That's far too many, but that is the American way. They order too much food, they leave too much food, they use too much gas, and their president is a plastic-headed buffoon. But these pancakes are good, and are America's gift to the world, along with permission to turn right on a red light.

MAKES 12–16 PANCAKES
PREP TIME: 10 MINUTES
COOKING TIME: 15 MINUTES

175g/6oz/1¼ cups self-raising
  (self-rising) flour
1 tsp baking powder
1 tsp bicarbonate of soda
  (baking soda)
A pinch of salt
50g/1¾oz/¼ cup
  caster sugar
A US Marines-sized knob
  of butter, plus extra
  for cooking
2 medium eggs, beaten
300ml/10fl oz/1¼ cups
  buttermilk
Milk (optional)
Fried bacon rashers and
  maple syrup, to serve

TIP: if you don't have
buttermilk you can make
your own before you start
preparing the pancake mix.
Pour 300ml/10fl oz/1¼ cups
milk into a jug and add 2½
tbsp lemon juice. Stir well
and leave to one side for
30 minutes.

Using a sieve, sift together the flour, baking powder and bicarbonate of soda into a bowl, with a pinch of salt. Then stir in the sugar.

Melt the butter in a pan. Whisk together the eggs, buttermilk and melted butter in a small bowl. Then gradually whisk in the flour to make a smooth, fairly thick batter. If it's too thick add a drop of milk.

Leave it to stand and cool for 5 minutes.

Now brace yourself.

Heat a large non-stick frying pan over a medium heat. When really hot, brush the surface with a li'l bit of butter.

Pour about 2 tablespoons of your pancake mixture into the pan, so it forms a 10-cm/4-inch circle.

Cook for around 2–3 minutes. Little holes will start to pop open on the upper surface, like a moonscape.

Flip it over and cook the other side until golden and set. Remove the pancake and place on a warmed plate.

Keep going with further pancakes until you've used up all the batter. Layer them between sheets of kitchen roll so they don't stick together.

Serve with the fried bacon rashers and a drizzle of maple syrup. Disgusting. Alternatively, adorn with a selection of fruits, or Spam.

CHAPTER TWO
PASTA

SPAG BOL

If you learn to make one thing from this book, make it spag bol. I've never met anyone who doesn't like a good spag bol. Strictly, what is being made here is a ragù sauce, but 'Bolognese' has come to mean any meat and tomato sauce on pasta. Note the inclusion of red wine, less than half a bottle. The remainder can be used elsewhere, such as in your face.

SERVES 4
PREP TIME: 15 MINUTES
COOKING TIME: 40 MINUTES

2 tbsp olive oil
1 onion, peeled and
    finely chopped
2 carrots, peeled and diced
3 celery stalks, diced
2 garlic cloves, peeled
    and crushed
450g/1lb minced
    (ground) beef
2 tbsp tomato purée
300ml/10fl oz/1¼ cups
    red wine
1 x 400g/14oz can of
    chopped tomatoes
A few fresh thyme sprigs
450g/1lb spaghetti
4 tbsp freshly grated
    Parmesan cheese
Salt 'n' pepper

For the ragù sauce, first heat the oil in a large pan, add the onion, carrots and celery and fry until tender – around 5 minutes. Add the garlic and fry for another minute or two.

Now add the beef. Stir and cook until browned. Turn it over constantly with a spatula to break up any lumps. Stir in the tomato purée and wine, and bring to the boil.

Add the tomatoes and thyme, season with salt 'n' pepper, and bring back to the boil. Once boiling, reduce the heat and simmer for 20 minutes. If it looks too dry after a bit, add a tablespoonful of water. Should you add the lid? I suppose it depends on how runny it is. Lid management is worthy of a PhD.

While that's happening, put a large pan of salted water on to boil. Many people make the mistake of using a pan that is too small, which will make the pasta clag into a medieval building material. I use a whopper. When the water is boiling, add the spaghetti and cook for however long the packet suggests but taking off a minute or two to ensure the pasta is 'al dente', i.e. with a slight bite to it. Drain the pasta into a colander in the sink and give it a douse with cold water to stop it cooking any further. Return the spaghetti to the same pan.

Add the sauce to the pasta and mix well. Divide between warmed plates and serve sprinkled with Parmigiano Reggiano cheesiano.

LEFTOVER SPAGHETTI 'ROSTIS'

Spaghetti is the world's favourite pasta but that statistic may be born of our inability to cook the right amount. There's always some left over. So here's a use for it. If your leftover spag has formed into a solid block, well, you didn't cook it properly. Dunk it in boiling water and stir it around for a minute, and it should separate. Douse in cold water. The proportions below are theoretical: modify to suit the amount of leftover spag you have.

SERVES 1
PREP TIME: 10 MINUTES
COOKING TIME: 6 MINUTES

Leftover cooked spaghetti –
    about 150g/5½oz
3 anchovies in oil, chopped
1 tbsp pitted olives, chopped
1 tbsp capers, chopped
4 tbsp freshly grated
    Parmesan cheese
Pinch of dried chilli flakes
1 big or 2 medium
    eggs, beaten
2 tbsp olive oil
Black pepper

Chop the spaghetti into small pieces, about 1cm/½ inch long.

Mix together with the remaining ingredients, apart from the oil, and add some pepper.

Heat the oil in a large frying pan and then spoon in dollops of the spaghetti mix, squashing it down to form little cakes. Fry for around 3 minutes until crispy, then turn over and do the same on the other side.

Drain on kitchen roll and leave to cool for a bit.

Insert in face. They will still be too hot and your tongue will turn to pumice.

BEEF LASAGNE

When lasagne is well made, it exhibits a slight rigidity, so it can be sliced like a cake and the portions will stand up. Less well and it turns into a slop, but tastes exactly the same. Don't worry about it.

SERVES 4
PREP TIME: 15 MINS
COOKING TIME: 1 HOUR

For the size of dish to use, see page 15. We used an enamel baking dish.

1 tbsp olive oil
2 red onions, peeled and chopped
2 garlic cloves, peeled and crushed
500g/1lb 2oz minced (ground) beef
1 x 400g/14oz can of chopped tomatoes
A handful of flat-leaf parsley, chopped
6–8 dried lasagne sheets
4 tbsp freshly grated Parmesan cheese
Salt 'n' pepper

For the white sauce
50g/1¾oz/¼ cup butter
50g/1¾oz/⅓ cup flour
650ml/22fl oz/2¾ cups milk, at room temperature, not straight from the fridge
Freshly grated nutmeg

Heat the oil in a large frying pan, add the onion and cook until it softens – around 4 minutes. Then add the garlic and cook for a further 5 minutes, stirring.

Add the minced beef and fry until brown. Turn it over constantly with a spatula to break up any lumps.

Now add the tomatoes and seasoning and cook for 30 minutes. Stir in the chopped parsley and let it cool.

Preheat the oven to 200ºC/400ºF.

For the white sauce, melt the butter in a medium saucepan but without burning it. Whisk in the flour a little at a time, stirring until it's well incorporated. It should stick together but not quite form a ball. Cook for a few minutes, whisking constantly, so the flour cooks out.

Now gradually whisk in the milk, a little at a time, until it thickens. Keep stirring, then add some freshly grated nutmeg.

In your baking dish, layer the meat sauce, pasta, more meat sauce, then white sauce, then add more layers, finishing with white sauce. Trim and arrange the pasta sheets so there are no ugly bits sticking out.

Anoint the top with the cheese and bake for 30 minutes until the top is golden brown.

HOW TO PIMP YOUR BASIC WHITE SAUCE

The standard white sauce, as used in the lasagne recipes, is a great starting point for devilish experimentation worthy of Dr Jekyll. Anything is worth a shot; here are a few standards.

Cheese sauce Stir in a Farmhouse Cheddar or Gruyère cheese, or even combine a few. Add a pinch of English mustard powder for heartburn.

Mushroom sauce Finely slice any old mushrooms, fry them gently in oil or add them to the sauce as it cooks.

Onion sauce As above but using a very finely diced onion.

Parsley sauce Chop up proper parsley into very tiny pieces (a good job for the wheelie herb chopper, see page 54) and mix in while cooking. Great with ham and mash with peas.

Spam sauce Grate in half a block of Spam during the cooking process and use as an accompaniment to Spam.

Go mad...

LENTIL & AUBERGINE LASAGNE

Our witless and trusting bovine chums will thank you for making this vegetarian interpretation of the stratified minced beef, pasta and sauce standard. This version is better than you might think. Chop the aubergine and pepper very thoroughly in the 'chopper upperer' (see page 37) as you want a nice dense filling. Be meticulous about trimming your pasta sheets to fit your oven dish. You don't want any crusty bits sticking out.

SERVES 4
PREP TIME: 15 MINUTES
COOKING TIME: 1 HOUR

For the size of dish to use, see page 15. We used an enamel baking dish.

1 tbsp olive oil
2 red onions, peeled and chopped
2 garlic cloves, peeled and crushed
2 aubergines (eggplants), roughly chopped
1 red (bell) pepper, deseeded and chopped
1 x 400g/14oz can of chopped tomatoes
1 x 400g/14oz can of green lentils, drained
A handful of flat-leaf parsley, chopped
6–8 dried lasagne sheets
4 tbsp freshly grated Parmesan cheese

For the white sauce
50g/1¾oz/¼ cup butter
50g/1¾oz/⅓ cup flour
650ml/22fl oz/2¾ cups milk, at room temperature, not straight from the fridge
Freshly grated nutmeg

Heat the oil in a large frying pan, add the onion and cook until it softens – around 4 minutes. Then add the garlic and cook for a further 5 minutes. Keep stirring, you halfwit.

Add the aubergine and cook for another 5 minutes, until it starts to go brown. Throw in the pepper, tomatoes and lentils. Season and cook gently for 30 minutes. If the mixture becomes a bit dry, add a splash of water. Once cooked, stir in the chopped parsley and let it cool.

Preheat the oven to 200ºC/400ºF.

To make the white sauce, melt the butter in a medium saucepan without letting it burn, then whisk in the flour, a little at a time, stirring until it's well incorporated. It should stick together but not quite form a ball. Cook for a few minutes, whisking constantly, so the flour cooks out.

Slowly whisk in the milk, a little at a time, until it thickens. Keep stirring, then add in some freshly grated nutmeg.

In your baking dish, layer the veg sauce, followed by pasta, followed by more veg sauce, followed by white sauce. Add another layer of pasta and then repeat the layers, finishing with the white sauce. Trim and arrange the pasta sheets so there are no ugly bits sticking out.

Scatter the cheese on top and bake for 30 minutes until the top is golden brown.

Serve on plates with cutlery. [!]

PENNE CARBONARA

The key to getting this right is not to overcook the pasta and not to scramble the egg and cheese mixture. The cream is optional and, personally, I would never use it, because I'm not a chav. You don't have to use penne – I just like the way the juice disappears into the tubes. Spaghetti is traditionally more 'correct'. You can also use Spam instead of pancetta, or for a vegetarian version, use chopped exotic mushrooms and rennet-free cheese.

SERVES 4
PREP TIME: 10 MINUTES
COOKING TIME: 12 MINUTES

1 tbsp olive oil
140g/5oz smoked
   pancetta lardons
2 egg yolks and 1 whole egg
4 tbsp Parmesan cheese,
   finely grated, plus extra
   for serving
100ml/3½fl oz/scant ½ cup
   double (heavy) cream
   (optional and not
   recommended)
300g/10½oz dried
   penne pasta
A handful of flat-leaf
   parsley, chopped
Salt 'n' pepper

Put a frying pan on the heat. Add the oil and smoked pancetta and cook until the pancetta becomes a bit crispy at the edges – around 4 minutes.

Remove from the pan and set aside to drain on a sheet of kitchen roll.

Add the eggs, most of the grated Parmesan cheese and a good grind of black pepper to a bowl and mix. This is where you would add the cream if you really must, you peasant. Stir smoothly but don't whisk. Set to one side.

Cook the penne in a large pan of salted boiling water, and however long the packet suggests, knock a minute or two off the time. This will ensure your pasta is 'al dente', i.e. with a slight bite to it.

Drain the pasta into a colander in the sink and give it a douse with cold water from the tap to stop it cooking any further.

Return the pasta to the hot pan and place on a very low heat to dry off the pasta for 15 seconds or so. Add the pancetta and stir.

Now for the difficult bit. Remove the pan from the heat and, stirring continuously, pour in the egg 'n' cheese mixture. It should turn a bit granular but should not scramble.

Spoon into warmed bowls, sprinkle with the remaining Parmesan cheese and garnish with parsley for appearances.

Pepper grinders
are becoming
far too elaborate

PASTA
WITH ANCHOVIES & TOMATOES

You can make this with any regular pasta, but it looks especially convincing with spaghetti. You can increase the amount of garlic if you like it that way, but I find it can overpower the subtlety of the anchovies.

SERVES 4
PREP TIME: 15 MINUTES
COOKING TIME: 25 MINUTES

1 x 50g/1¾oz can of anchovy fillets in oil
1 medium onion, peeled and finely chopped
4 garlic cloves, peeled and crushed
1 tbsp tomato purée
1 x 400g/14oz can of chopped tomatoes
500g/1lb 2oz spaghetti or whatevs
125g/4½oz/⅔ cup black olives, pitted and chopped
A large handful flat-leaf parsley, chopped
Salt 'n' pepper

Pour just the oil from the can of anchovies into a medium pan, heat it up, add the onion and garlic and cook for 5 minutes.

Add the anchovies and tomato purée and cook, stirring, for 1 minute. Use a spatula to chop each anchovy fillet into three, for better dispersal through the sauce.

Add the tomatoes, bring to the boil and simmer for 15 minutes. Season with salt and pepper.

Meanwhile, cook the pasta in a large pan of lightly salted water. Follow the packet timings but knock a minute off if you like your pasta to be 'al dente', i.e. there is still a slight bite to it. Drain.

Stir the chopped olives into the sauce, then pour the sauce onto the pasta.

Toss it around in the pan so the pasta is well coated with the sauce.

Serve garnished with the chopped parsley.

Say, 'I once went to the River Café, you know.'

CHAPTER THREE

PUB GRUB

STEAK 'N' FRIES

This recipe is for two people, as it's long been held that the ability to turn out a good steak is the true mark of an eligible man or woman, and this should therefore be thought of as extended foreplay. The chances of success are medium to rare.

SERVES 2
PREP TIME: 10 MINUTES
COOKING TIME: 20–30 MINUTES

350g/12oz sweet potatoes
Olive oil, to drizzle
Leaves stripped from a few fresh rosemary sprigs and thyme sprigs
2 x 200g/7oz sirloin steaks
Mushrooms and cherry tomatoes to grill, if you remember, or serve with cooked frozen peas as a last-minute 'save the day' option
Salt 'n' pepper

Preheat the oven to 200ºC/400ºF.

Wash the sweet potatoes, scrubbing them with a nail brush if necessary, but you don't need to peel them. Cut them into wedges, not too thick. Arrange them, spaced out, on a roasting pan, and drizzle some olive oil over them.

Sprinkle the rosemary and thyme around the wedges, grind some black pepper on top and finish off with a light swathe of salt.

Cook in the oven for 20–30 minutes, turning occasionally, until golden brown and 'pub-ish'.

Meanwhile, place a griddle pan (or a thick-bottomed regular frying pan) over a high heat.

Rub both sides of the steaks with a little olive oil and season with salt (sea salt crystals, if you have them). Do not oil the pan.

When the pan is really hot and on the verge of melting, add the steaks and cook for 2–3 minutes per side (rare), 4–5 minutes (medium) or 5–6 minutes (well done).

Obviously, exactly how long each steak takes depends on its thickness, age and so on. There are techniques for poking steaks with your finger to assess how well they're cooked, but as a beginner cook, just cut a bit off the end and see how it looks.

Eat this bit. Make sure you serve that steak to yourself, because the missing bit will be noticed.

When the steaks are done, remove from the pan and rest for a few minutes before serving, along with the sweet potato wedges and the steak juices from the pan.

While the steaks were cooking, you could have lightly grilled some comedically large mushrooms and a few cherry tomatoes as an accompaniment. But you forgot. So you can save the day by quickly cooking some frozen peas. Do this in the steak pan with a splash of the red wine you've been drinking throughout this.

Vegetarians can simply omit the steak

COTTAGE PIE

It's quite difficult to mess this up. There is huge latitude in the ingredients and cooking technique for this potato-topped pie, and so long as you come out with something meaty and juicy with potato on top, you can claim success. This is a cottage pie, because it's made with beef. A shepherd's pie is exactly the same, but with lamb. I've also tried making a vegetarian version with Quorn vegetarian mince. It tasted like reconstituted social services jobs pages from The Guardian.

SERVES 4
PREP TIME: 15 MINUTES
COOKING TIME: 1 HOUR

1 tbsp olive oil
1 medium onion, peeled
    and chopped
2 carrots, peeled and diced
1 small red chilli, finely chopped
450g/1lb minced (ground) beef
1 tbsp flour
450ml/16fl oz/scant 2 cups
    hot beef stock
3 tbsp tomato purée
2 tbsp Worcestershire sauce
A large handful of frozen peas
1kg/2lb 4oz floury potatoes,
    peeled and chopped
4–5 tbsp milk
A decent knob of butter
Salt 'n' pepper

Preheat the oven to 200ºC/400ºF.

Heat the oil in a large, deep frying pan. Add the onion and carrot and cook gently until softened – around 3-4 minutes. Add the chilli and cook for a further 2 minutes.

Add the beef, stirring well, until the meat is broken up and browned all over.

Stir in the flour, a little at a time, very thoroughly. Then add the hot stock and tomato purée and bring to the boil. Reduce the heat to a simmer.

Add the Worcestershire sauce and peas, season with salt and pepper, cover the pan, and cook for around 15 minutes. The juice should thicken up.

While you're doing all this, cook the potatoes in a large pan of boiling salted water until soft, which will take around 20 minutes.

Drain, add the milk and butter and mash until smooth. Season to taste.

Spoon the meat mixture into a large ovenproof dish. Cover with mashed potato. Use a fork to make a corrugated pattern on top.

Cook in the oven until the top is golden brown – around 25 minutes.

FISH PIE

This makes enough to fill two pub-style individual earthenware dishes, for that authentic local boozer experience. You can double up the quantities for four. Please bear in mind that my fish pie is, officially, better than Gordon Ramsay's.

SERVES 2
PREP TIME: 15 MINUTES
COOKING TIME: 35 MINUTES

For the potato topping
450g/1lb floury
    potatoes, peeled
    and cubed
50ml/3 tbsp full fat
    (whole) milk
A decent knob of butter

For the filling
400g/14oz mixed selection
    of fish, e.g. smoked
    haddock, cod, salmon
    fillets and prawns
200ml/7fl oz/scant 1 cup
    full fat (whole) milk
A decent knob of butter
1 medium onion, peeled
    and chopped
1 leek, thinly sliced
1 tbsp flour
A handful of flat-leaf
    parsley, chopped
A handful of frozen peas,
    to decorate (optional)
Pepper

Preheat the oven to 200°C/400°F.

Cook the potatoes in a saucepan of boiling water until tender. Drain and mash with the milk and butter, until smooth. Season with a little black pepper.

Meanwhile, put the fish in a pan with the milk and heat until just coming to the boil. Reduce the heat and simmer for 5 minutes. Be careful not to overcook the fish.

Strain the fish and keep the fishy milk.

Melt the second knob of butter in a frying pan and cook the onion and leek over a low heat until soft and tender – around 10 minutes.

Stir the flour in, a little at a time, and cook for 1 minute. Now add the fishy milk, bit by bit, stirring all the time. The sauce will thicken. Add the cooked fish and the parsley. Season with pepper.

Divide the mixture between two dishes and cover evenly with mashed potato. Rough up the surface of the potato with a fork, for extra crispness.

Spell rude words on the top of your pie with frozen peas (optional).

Cook in the oven for 15–20 minutes, until the top is golden brown. Not the optional peas, though. They should still be green.

Sauce overspill
proves it's not
a ready meal

HALF & HALF PIE

This pie satisfies carnivores and veggies alike, all in the same pie dish. You could make two pies but it's not as clever. Also, if you're cooking for carnivores only, the other half of the pie could be the vegetables. We've had pie 'n' peas, this is pie 'n' pie. There's nothing not to like. I used an enamelware pie dish approximately 22cm/8½ inch diameter and 5cm/2 inches deep.

SERVES 4
PREP TIME: 30 MINUTES
COOKING TIME: 40 MINUTES

For the pie casing
500g/1lb 2oz pack of ready-made shortcrust pastry, at room temperature
Flour for dusting
1 egg, beaten, for glazing
Salt 'n' white pepper

For the chicken and mushroom half
2 tbsp vegetable oil
1 medium onion, peeled and cut into small bits
175g/6oz boneless, skinless chicken breast, cut into slightly bigger bits than the onion
175g/6oz mushrooms, sliced
½ x 295g/10oz can of condensed cream of mushroom soup

For the cheesy leek and potato half
250g/9oz potatoes, peeled and diced into 1-cm/½-inch cubes
1 large leek, sliced
A small knob of butter
90g/3¼oz Cheddar cheese, grated in the peerless Mouli

For the chicken and mushroom half

Heat the oil in a large frying pan, add the onion and cook gently for about 5 minutes until soft but not browned.

Add the chicken and mushrooms. Stir and cook for about 10 minutes until the mushrooms and chicken are cooked through.

Add the half can of soup and mix thoroughly.

Season to taste, then leave to cool. It's important that the mixture goes into the pie cold, otherwise it will melt the fats in the pastry and give you a soggy bottom.

For the cheesy leek and potato half

Clean your chicken spatula or use a different one.

Cook the potatoes in a pan of boiling, salted water for about 5 minutes until just starting to soften. Drain well.

Meanwhile, in a second pan gently fry the leek in the butter until soft, about 5–8 minutes.

Mix the potato and leek together and allow to cool, then add the cheese, stir well and season.

Assembly

This is the exciting part. Heat the oven to 190°C/375°F and put a baking sheet onto the middle shelf.

Cut the pastry block in half, then roll out each half on a floured surface into a circle large enough to cover the pie dish and about 5mm/¼ inch thick. Rotate the pastry as you roll, to keep it roughly circular. [JM: This pastry sounds a bit thick to me. Ed: 5mm is a pretty standard thickness.]

Take one circle and press one half of it into one half of the pie dish. Leave the other half flat and limp.

Fill the formed half with one of the fillings, spreading evenly. Now fold the other limp half over, moistening along the edge to seal it. Crimp with fingers or a fork. You are effectively making a Cornish pasty, and it should fill half of the pie dish. Trim off any overhanging pastry with a knife.

Repeat with the second circle and the second filling, making sure your two pasties abut each other in the dish.

Make a small slit in the top of each half so that the steam can escape. Use any scrap pastry to decorate the top if you wish to designate the veggie side and the chicken side. I used the letters C and V, obvs.

Brush the top of the pie with the beaten egg, then put onto the preheated baking sheet in the oven and cook for 35-40 minutes. If the pastry is beginning to get too brown, cover the pie with foil.

Remove from the oven and rest for 10 minutes before serving.

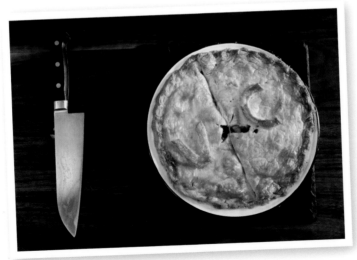

This pie(s) deserves a medal

CHILLI CON CARNE

This basic chilli recipe is a slow-cooked one. I have also made a vegan version with Meatless Farm meat-free mince, throwing in a couple of chopped whole chillies and a bit of garlic as well. The result was a successful chilli sans carne.

SERVES 4
PREP TIME: 5 MINUTES
COOKING TIME: 1 HOUR

2 tbsp olive oil
450g/1lb minced (ground) beef
1 large onion, peeled and
    finely chopped
1 tsp hot chilli powder
3 tbsp tomato purée
1 x 400g/14oz can of
    chopped tomatoes
300ml/10fl oz/1¼ cups
    hot beef stock
1 x 400g/14oz can of red kidney
    beans, drained and rinsed
1 bunch of fresh coriander
    (cilantro), chopped
Salt 'n' pepper

WHEELIE HERB CHOPPER

How it works Four circular and rotating blades extend from the body when you turn a knob. Push the chopper around over herbs to slice.

For Quick, effective, strangely pleasing.

Against Almost impossible to sharpen.

Destination Knife drawer.

Heat half the oil in a non-stick frying pan and cook the mince, not too quickly, until well browned and any lumps have broken up. Stir regularly.

While this is happening (if you dare, or do these as separate operations) heat the remaining oil in a nice big pan and cook the onion until soft. Add the chilli powder and cook for another minute.

Now add the cooked mince to this pan, followed by the tomato purée, the tomatoes and the hot stock.

Bring to the boil, then reduce the heat to a gentle simmer. Leave it like this for around 40 minutes, until the sauce is reduced and thick, stirring occasionally.

Five minutes before serving, bung in the beans and the coriander, stir well and cook for 5 minutes. Season with salt 'n' pepper.

Serve with rice and call each other 'Gringo', unless you aren't a Gringo.

LANCASHIRE HOT POT

*This is a much posher hotpot than any I ever ate as a student in Lancaster.
For a more low-rent version, use chopped up lamb's kidney instead of the
lamb, or Spam. I wouldn't, though.*

SERVES 4
PREP TIME: 20 MINUTES
COOKING TIME: 2 HOURS
AT LEAST

4 tbsp olive oil
12 lamb cutlets
2 medium onions,
    peeled and sliced
2–3 tsp flour (optional)
750ml/1¼ pints/3 cups hot
    lamb or vegetable stock
Leaves from 2 fresh
    thyme sprigs
2 large carrots,
    peeled and sliced
450g/1lb floury potatoes,
    such as King Edward
    or Maris Piper, sliced
2 tbsp butter
Salt 'n' pepper

Preheat the oven to 180ºC/375ºF. Put a large lidded casserole
in the oven to heat up.

Meanwhile, add the oil to a large frying pan and fry the cutlets
on both sides to brown them off a bit. You might need to do this
in stages depending on the size of your pan. Remove them from
the pan with a slotted spoon and set aside.

Now soften the onions in the same pan, but not too much –
4-5 minutes should be enough. Don't let them brown.

Take the hot casserole from the oven and chuck the lamb
and onions into it. Stir in a couple of teaspoons of flour if
you want a thicker sauce, and add the stock. Add the thyme
leaves and a bit o' seasoning.

Put the lid on this lot and shove it back in the oven for around
30 minutes.

Remove the casserole from the oven. Stir in the sliced carrots.
Now layer the sliced potatoes over the top, so that they overlap
attractively and cover the whole area.

Put the lid back on and stick it back in the oven for an hour.

Take it back out of the oven. Turn the oven up to 230ºC/450ºF.
Dot the butter over the top of the potato layer, then put it back
in the oven, without the lid on, for another 30 minutes, or until
the potatoes are crisp and golden.

Serve and talk about trouble at t' mill.

BAKED TROUT
WITH NEW POTS 'N' PEAS

I've made this for two people, as it's a great seduction dish and will make you look sophisticated, even though it's easy. The only skill required is in not overdoing the fish. The flesh should be pink throughout but still moist. If you're not confident of doing surgery on a whole fish, you could buy fillets. The result is not as impressive, though.

SERVES 2
PREP TIME: 15 MINUTES
COOKING TIME: 20 MINUTES

2 fresh trout, gutted, but
   heads and tails still on
2 sprigs of fresh rosemary
A small knob of butter
2 handfuls of small
   new potatoes
1 teacupful of frozen peas
Creamed horseradish
   sauce, to serve
Salt

Preheat the oven to 180°C/360°F.

Rinse the fish in cold water, making sure to sluice any crud out of its guts. Pat dry with kitchen roll. Place each one on a rectangle of foil large enough to make a parcel. Push the rosemary into the gut cavity. Put a smear of butter on top of each one and a tiny sprinkle of salt. Make a parcel of each fish by folding the foil up lengthways and crimping it over. Then fold up the ends. Put the parcels on a baking sheet near the top of the oven.

Now put your spuds in a pan of lightly salted cold water and start bringing them to the boil. Once boiling, they should take around 20 minutes and should be ready at the same time as the fish.

Decant the peas into a bowl and set aside.

How long the fish will take to cook depends on the size of the fish. After 20 minutes, partly unwrap the bigger fish and stick a sharp knife into the fattest bit to ease the flesh apart. It should be turning pink. If not, give it a few more minutes. Unfold the parcels and cook for another 5 minutes exposed to the heat.

Your potatoes should now be done. Strain and return to the hot pan to dry out.

Pour boiling water on the peas and leave for a few minutes. This will cook them enough.

Lift the fish onto warmed plates. Arrange the potatoes artfully. Pour the fishy/herby/buttery juice from the parcels over everything. Drain the peas and add to the plates.

Serve with a discreet blob of creamed horseradish sauce.

Explain to your victim how you once went fly fishing but the fish weren't 'rising'. This will make you sound like a proper nob.

BEAN CASSOULET

I once ate something like this in a roadside café when cycling through France many years ago. I'm glad I was on a bicycle in the open air, and not in a car. To make it vegetarian, use mushrooms or chopped aubergine instead of the bacon lardons.

SERVES 4
PREP TIME: 15 MINUTES
COOKING TIME: 50 MINUTES

1 tbsp olive oil
225g/8oz bacon lardons
1 medium onion, peeled
 and chopped
2 red (bell) peppers,
 deseeded and chopped
1 x 400g/14oz can of
 chopped tomatoes
A pinch of dried chilli flakes
2 x 400g/14oz cans of mixed
 beans, drained and rinsed
A large handful of flat-leaf
 parsley, chopped
Salt 'n' pepper

Heat the oil in a large pan and cook the lardons until golden – around 5 minutes. Remove them from the pan with a slotted spoon and put them to one side.

Chuck the onion and peppers into the same pan and cook in the bacony oil for 10 minutes, or until soft.

Put the lardons back in, plus the tomatoes, chilli flakes and 200ml/7fl oz/scant 1 cup of water. Bring to the boil, then reduce the heat and simmer for 20 minutes, stirring occasionally. Put the lid on, if you are worried about it drying out.

Now add the beans, with trembling hand, and cook for another 10 minutes.

Stir in the chopped parsley and season to taste.

Open the window.

MULTI SCISSORS

How it works Like a pair of scissors, four times over, simultaneously.

For Intriguing.

Against Looking at them makes you feel drunk.

Destination Re-gifting pile. (In truth, we found these really useful during the TV filming.)

RATATOUILLE

There are many versions of ratatouille, a southern French invention. This simple version can be considered as a jumping-off point for your own adaptations – by rights, it should always contain aubergine, courgette and peppers. My recipe uses fresh basil but I've also tried it with fennel, and I don't see why you couldn't use any fresh green herbs. It's easy to make but impossible to spell.

SERVES 4
PREP TIME: 20 MINUTES
COOKING TIME: 45 MINUTES

5 tbsp olive oil
2 medium onions, peeled
   and thinly sliced
2 garlic cloves, peeled
   and crushed
1 aubergine (eggplant), cubed
450g/1lb courgettes (zucchini),
   thinly sliced
450g/1lb tomatoes, peeled
   and roughly chopped
1 green and 1 red (bell) pepper,
   deseeded and sliced
4 tbsp chopped fresh basil,
   or whatevs
2 tbsp tomato purée
A handful of chopped
   flat-leaf parsley, to garnish
Salt 'n' pepper

Add the oil, onions and garlic to a large pan and gently fry for 4–5 minutes until the onions are soft.

Add everything else to the pan except the parsley. Season. Cook for 5–6 minutes, with the occasional stir.

Simmer gently until all the vegetables are just tender, which should be around 30 minutes. If the ratatouille now looks a bit watery, you can tip a bit of the juice out when no-one's looking, or you can simmer for longer and allow it to thicken. But this might make the ingredients more mushy. Some people like it mushy, others prefer it crunchy. You can decide at this point how you want it. I admit a fondness for a slightly mushy one.

Sprinkle with parsley. The ratatouille can be served hot or chilled, but chilled is a bit crap.

Talk about how much you used to enjoy listening to Peter Mayle's *A Year in Provence* on BBC Radio 4.

CHAPTER FOUR
ROASTS

ROAST CHICKEN

There are countless theories about roasting a chicken: cover with foil, don't cover with foil, cover with foil but take it off 20 minutes before the end, blast it, then turn it down, shove an opened can of lager up its arse (Australian), blah blah blah. I've tried most of them – this is the simplest method, and it works.

SERVES 4
PREP TIME: BLOODY AGES
COOKING TIME: 1 HOUR
15 MINUTES

125g/4½oz/½ cup butter, at room temperature
5 tbsp chopped fresh lemon thyme, plus extra sprigs
1 x 1.5kg/3lb 5oz free-range or organic chicken
1 lemon, juice squeezed out and halves reserved
1 large onion, peeled and halved
Salt 'n' pepper

Preheat the oven to 190ºC/375ºF. Place a roasting pan in the oven.

Blend the butter and chopped lemon thyme in a bowl, seasoning generously.

Ease your fingers under the skin of the chicken at the neck end and tease it away from the flesh. You're making a space for the herb butter mix.

Push the herb butter under the skin, spreading it around evenly. Keep a teaspoon's worth in reserve.

Place the chicken the obvious way up in the hot roasting pan. Rub the reserved teaspoon of herb butter all over the breasts and thighs.

Pour the lemon juice over the top. Shove the lemon and onion halves inside the carcass.

Roast in the oven for 1 hour and 15 minutes, or until the skin is a golden colour. Check it's cooked properly by shoving the point of a small knife into the fat part of the thigh. The juices should run completely clear.

If the chicken looks to be drying out during roasting, spoon some of the juices from the pan over the top.

When it's definitely done, remove from the oven and let it rest for 15 minutes before carving. You can make the gravy while the chicken rests.

Steal one of the wings, 'to check it's done'.

Say 'I'll carve the bird' in a pompous and declamatory fashion.

Now wield your expensive or ancestral carving knife and fork with much theatre, despite ultimately creating the impression that the job was done by the local council with a rotavator.

BASIC GRAVY

Gravy is a luxury commodity, symbolic of bloated decadence and excess. It's why we have the expression 'the gravy train'. In truth, it is made with nothing more than the effluent of the roasting process.

PREP TIME: 2 MINUTES
COOKING TIME: 2–3 MINUTES

Hot fat and meat juices
    from the roast chicken
300–400ml/10–14fl oz/1½ cups
    vegetable water or vegetable
    or chicken stock
Pinch o' salt

Pour all the fat from the bottom of the chicken roasting pan into a saucepan, leaving behind any sediment. Place the pan over a medium heat and add the stock and the salt. Stir well, scraping up any gunk from the bottom of the pan, and boil until the gravy is as rich and brown as Richard Hammond on his holidays.

If you want to thicken the gravy (technically making it a sauce) mix a tablespoon of flour with a mug of cold water and stir to a runny paste. Pour into the gravy a bit at a time, whisking, until the flour is cooked out.

If you're drinking a sturdy red wine with the roast chicken – and you should be – you could throw a couple of teaspoons of that in as well. Cook for a further few minutes.

Serve hot in a ludicrous 'boat' that you bought many years ago when you still thought you could appear sophisticated.

BEST CHICKEN STOCK

Don't throw away your chicken carcass. It makes delicious stock which can be the basis of many a good nourishing soup. While the stock is simmering away you can get on with life's other pleasures, such as reading the complete works of John Keats.

PREP TIME: 10 MINUTES
COOKING TIME: 2 ½ HOURS

1 leftover roast chicken
    carcass, including the
    lemon and onion halves
225g/8oz onions, 150g/5oz
    leeks, 225g/8oz celery
    sticks, roughly chopped
2 bay leaves, a few sprigs
    of thyme, a small
    handful of parsley
½ tsp salt

Put all the ingredients in a large saucepan and add 3 litres/5 pints of cold water. Cover the pan, bring slowly to the boil and skim the surface of any scum with a slotted spoon.

Partially cover the pan, reduce the heat and simmer gently for 2 hours. Skim occasionally if necessary. Check the seasoning.

Strain the stock through a sieve into a bowl and cool quickly. Cover and keep in the fridge for up to 3 days. Before using remove the solid layer of fat from the surface with a metal spatula and discard.

YORKSHIRE PUDDINGS

Yorkshires are best served straight out of the oven, when they're all puffed up like a local politician. That means you need to think carefully about timing here, so they're ready just as you're about to carve your chicken. You'll almost certainly balls this up. You will need a 12-bun baking sheet.

MAKES 12 SMALL PUDDINGS
PREP TIME: 10 MINUTES
COOKING TIME: 20–25 MINUTES

3 big eggs and equal quantities
   of flour and milk
½ tsp salt
4 tbsp sunflower oil

Heat the oven to 220ºC/430ºF.

Crack the eggs into a jug and then measure out the same volume of flour and milk.

Mix the flour and salt together in a big bowl and make a well in the centre.

Add the eggs and a little bit of the milk. Whisk until smooth, then gradually add the remaining milk, still whisking. Pour this mixture into a jug with a spout. This is now your batter.

Pour a teaspoon of oil into each bun hole. Put the baking sheet in the oven for around 5 minutes. The oil must be well hot.

Take the sheet from the oven and swiftly divide the batter equally between the bun holes.

Return the sheet to the oven immediately and cook for 20–25 minutes, until the puddings are golden brown and well risen.

Say 'ta-daaa' as you reveal them, for it is indeed magic.

ROAST POTATOES

Sir Walter Raleigh may have blighted society with tobacco and the Chopper bicycle, but he also brought us potatoes, without which we wouldn't have roasties. Roasties are dead easy. If you can't manage this you should consider volunteering to wash up instead.

SERVES 4
PREP TIME: 12 MINUTES
COOKING TIME: 50 MINUTES

1kg/2lb 4oz floury spuds,
    e.g. Maris Piper or
    King Edward
100g/3½oz goose or duck fat,
    or dripping, or vegetable
    oil if vegetarian
Some salt

Preheat the oven to 190ºC/375ºF.

Peel the potatoes and cut into quarters (if big 'uns) or halves if smaller. It's best to have roughly even-sized pieces.

Put them in a saucepan and cover with cold water. Bring to the boil and cook for around 5 minutes, until they begin to yield to the point of a knife.

Meanwhile, put the fat or oil into a roasting pan and heat it up in the oven.

Drain the potatoes well in a colander. You now need to rough them up a bit. Either shake the colander vigorously so the potatoes become a bit fluffy around the edges, or run the tines of a fork around each one.

Remove the roasting pan from the oven. It will be unbelievably hot. Tip the potatoes into the hot fat and roll them around so they're coated all over.

Roast for around 25 minutes. Then remove them from the oven and turn them all over using a 'gazunder' of some sort or a large, slotted spoon. Return to the oven and cook for another 25 minutes.

You'll know when they're done. You know what a roast potato looks like.

Beetroot Not worth the bother.

Broccoli Slice up around 1cm/1/2 inch below the bulbous bit. Separate the florets by cutting lengthways and slice big 'uns in half.

Brussels sprouts Trim the base and remove any sad-looking outer leaves. Now, do you cut a cross in the base or not? It's supposed to help tenderise that tough bit, but it may be an old wives' tale by now. Chop over-large sprouts in half.

Cabbage and related leaves Pull off any ugly outer leaves. Slice off the base and trim out the inner 'heart'. Slice the surviving leaves coarsely, or shred them with a sharp knife.

Carrots Chop off the root end. Peel. Now what? Circles are comforting, batons are considered more sophisticated. The British army just randomly bayonets them into chunks.

Cauliflower Discard the leaves, carve out the woody core and separate into florets.

Celery Cut off the root and the fluffy bit at the opposite end. Contemplate for a few seconds and then transfer to bin.

Green beans, runner beans Top and tail (i.e. cut the ends off) and pull out any stringy bits. Slice runner beans at an angle or push them through an ancestral slicer. Some people strip off the outer edge of runner beans but life's a bit short.

Kale This is not actually food, just an affectation.

Leeks Cut off the root and the tough upper leaves. Gently slice lengthways and remove the outer layer. Slice into circles.

Mangetout Top and tail, unless very fresh.

Parsnips As for carrots, but always cut lengthways.

Peas Split the pods and nudge the peas out with a finger or thumb. Alternatively, take from packet in freezer.

Spinach and chard Rinse and pat dry, cut any fleshy stems from the leaves and slice the leaves and stalks.

Swede (rutabaga) and turnip Cut off the root, peel, chop up for par-boiling prior to mashing or roasting.

STEAMED VEGETABLES

For some reason, steamed veg tastes nicer than veg boiled in a saucepan. You will need a steamer, but if you don't have one, you can improvise with a saucepan, a sieve and a tight-fitting lid. Every single vegetable ever to spring from the loins of our bountiful earth has been a unique size and shape, so the only way to know if veg is done is to pick a piece out and try it. I like my veg firm and crunchy but some people like them as if steamed since the end of rationing.

PREP TIME: 5 MINUTES

Vegetables
Water

TIMES FOR STEAMING VEG

Here is my rough guide
to cooking times for
firm textures:

Broccoli
4 minutes
Brussels sprouts
10 mins
Cabbage and related leaves
5 minutes
Carrots
8 minutes
Cauliflower
9 minutes
Green beans, runner beans
4 minutes
Leeks
7 minutes
Mangetout (snow peas)
4 minutes
Peas
3 minutes
Spinach and chard
3 minutes
Spam
15 minutes

Peel (if necessary) and chop your veg (see facing page).

Add water to the lower pan and bring to the boil. You can start with boiling water for this. Only root vegetables that grow below ground should be brought to the boil from cold. (I bet not many of you know that.)

Now make a mental plan. The longest-steaming vegetable should go in the top level first, and others added in the right order so that they are co-terminus. This is easier with a multi-level dedicated steamer.

When the veg are done, remove the sieve or top section from the steamer, shake it about and let it stand for around 30 seconds so that any excess moisture evaporates.

Decanting the cooked veg into warmed bowls or oven dishes is a good idea. This makes them look nice, and you can even add garnishes.

CAULIFLOWER CHEESE

For a youth growing up in the 1970s, cauliflower cheese was an event in itself. Better still, when we went out as a family for Sunday lunch, once a year, it was a surprise accompaniment at the carvery. It is in that spirit that it is presented here. A large portion is a suitable alternative to the roast chicken if you have vegetarian guests, and it's just as good. You can make this while the chicken is roasting in the oven.

SERVES 4
PREP TIME: 20 MINUTES
COOKING TIME: 40 MINUTES

1 large cauliflower,
   leaves and stalk removed,
   cut into florets
50g/1¾oz/[1/4] cup butter,
   plus extra for greasing
50g/1¾oz/[1/3] flour
500ml/18fl oz/2 cups milk,
   at room temperature, not
   straight from the fridge
150g/5½oz mature Cheddar
   cheese, finely grated
½ tsp boggo mustard
   (optional)
Salt (optional) 'n' pepper

Preheat the oven to 200ºC/400ºF.

Lightly grease a shallow ovenproof dish with butter.

Half fill a large saucepan with water and bring to the boil. Add the cauliflower florets and boil for 8-10 minutes. The cauliflower should be hot throughout but still quite crunchy. Try a bit.

Drain the cauliflower, blast with cold water to stop it cooking further and set aside.

Meanwhile, melt the butter in a medium saucepan over a low heat without letting it burn and gradually whisk in the flour, a little at a time, until it forms a smooth paste that will almost form into a ball. Don't create a building material.

Cook this mixture for a few minutes, whisking constantly, so the flour cooks out. Still over the heat, whisk in the milk a bit at a time. This way you won't get any lumps.

Keep cooking and stirring until the sauce has thickened enough to coat the back of a spoon - around 6–8 minutes.

Stir in the grated cheese, still over a low heat. Do a taste test and add some mustard for extra zing if desired. Season with salt, if needed, and pepper.

Arrange the cauliflower florets in the ovenproof dish and pour the cheesy sauce all over, making sure none of the cauliflower is left naked.

Bake for 20-25 minutes, until the top is turning slightly brown and bubbling.

Consume and descend into a cheese coma.

NUT ROAST

This is one of the biggest clichés in cooking. The early vegetarians of my student days were offered nothing else, because catering for vegetarians was still seen as a massive inconvenience. So it was whatever everyone else was having, plus a nut roast for that veggie weirdo. As a result, it has been stigmatised. A shame, because a good one is great. I hope you think this is such.

SERVES 4
PREP TIME: 30 MINUTES
COOKING TIME: 40 MINUTES

2 tbsp olive oil
1 onion, peeled and chopped
2 garlic cloves, peeled and
    finely chopped
250g/9oz boggo mushrooms,
    finely chopped
150g/5½oz/1½ cups shelled
    pistachios, chopped
150g/5½oz walnuts, chopped
1 medium egg, beaten
100g/3½oz/2 cups
    breadcrumbs made
    from toast
50g/1¾oz/½ cup
    pumpkin seeds
1 tsp chopped fresh thyme
½ tsp chopped
    fresh rosemary
1 tbsp soy sauce
A small handful of
    flat-leaf parsley,
    chopped, to garnish

Preheat the oven to 180°C/350°F.

Line the bottom of a medium loaf tin or similar with baking parchment.

Heat the oil in a frying pan and soften the onion for 5 minutes. Add the garlic and mushrooms and cook for another 5 minutes. Transfer this mixture to a bowl.

Add the chopped nuts and mix. Then add the egg, breadcrumbs, pumpkin seeds, thyme, rosemary and soy sauce. Mix together well and season.

Tip the whole lot into the loaf tin and pat down to even it out, but not too firmly.

Roast in the oven for 30–40 minutes, or until set into a loaf. Allow to stand for 5 minutes before turning out and cutting into slices. Garnish with chopped parsley.

If the nut roast seems too dry, smother it with rich, beefy gravy.

CHAPTER FIVE

CURRY NIGHT

CHICKEN CHEATER MASALA

This isn't a true tikka masala ('masala' simply means a mixture of spices), because to do that you'd have to cook the chicken pieces on skewers in a tandoor. But it's a pretty good fake. As this is a big and complicated job, I've made it for six people. If you're going to make this much effort, you want it to be appreciated. It might be a good idea to start this the day before.

SERVES 6
PREP TIME: 24 HOURS
COOKING TIME: 30 MINUTES

800g/1lb 12oz chicken breasts, boneless, skinless, cut into fork-sized chunks
A handful of fresh coriander (cilantro) leaves, to garnish

For the marinade
150g/5oz (small pot) plain yoghurt
4 garlic cloves, peeled and crushed
5cm/2 inch piece of ginger, peeled and finely sliced
2 tbsp garam masala
1 tsp ground turmeric
1 tsp chilli powder
1 tsp ground cumin
A pinch of salt

For the sauce
2 tbsp vegetable oil
A large knob of butter
1 large onion, peeled and diced
3 garlic cloves, peeled and crushed
5cm/2 inch piece of ginger, peeled and grated
1½ tsp garam masala
1½ tsp ground cumin
1 tsp ground turmeric
1 tsp ground coriander
½ tsp black cardamom seeds, crushed
400ml/14fl oz/1¾ cups tomato passata
1 tsp chilli powder
a pinch of salt
250ml/9fl oz/1 cup double (heavy) cream
1 tsp brown sugar

Bung all the marinade ingredients into a bowl and stir together.

Make small cuts in your chicken chunks (this helps the marinade work its way in), add them to the marinade, mix all together and leave, covered, in the fridge overnight.

The next day

Preheat the oven to 160°C 325°F.

First, make the sauce.

Melt the oil and butter in a deep frying pan. Fry the onion until soft – around 4 minutes. Add the garlic and ginger. Stir around for a few minutes. It should start to smell fantastic.

Now add the garam masala, cumin, turmeric, ground coriander and black cardamom. Fry for another minute, stirring.

Pour in the passata, then add the chilli powder and salt. Bring to a simmer and keep on a low heat for around 20 minutes, stirring occasionally, until the juice thickens up.

Once the sauce is ready, keep it on a low heat, covered if necessary, while you prepare the chicken.

Remove the chicken pieces from the marinade, but keep the marinade.

Turn on the grill to a high temperature. Line the grill tray with foil and grill the chicken pieces, turning regularly, a few minutes on each side, until the surfaces are a rich, dark brown. At this stage you are cooking just the surfaces. The chicken will cook through completely in the sauce, later.

When the chicken is ready, add the leftover marinade, the cream and sugar to the sauce and stir together.

Now put the chicken pieces into the sauce and bring to a simmer. You need to cook the chicken through, which will take anything from 15–30 minutes, depending on the size of your pieces. Test a piece. There should be no pink meat inside.

Turn the masala into a serving dish and garnish with the coriander leaves.

Serve with basmati rice (see below) and the chapatis on page 86. Then have a long lie down.

COOKING BASMATI RICE

Basmati is a type of long grain rice and it's worth using it to get a good fluffy effect. Rinsing and soaking is not necessary but gives a lighter, more delicate texture.

450g/1lb/2 cups basmati rice
A pinch of salt

Toss the rice in a sieve under running water for a minute and then put it into a large pan and cover with cold water. Leave for at least 30 minutes.

Drain the rice and throw away the soaking water. Put the rice into a large pan on a medium heat with 600ml/1 pint of cold water and a generous pinch of salt.

Bring to the boil and give it a good stir. Cover tightly and reduce the heat to very low. Cook for 25 minutes, then take off the heat, place a dry tea towel over the pan, put the lid back on and place the pan to sit on a wet tea towel. Leave to stand for 5 minutes, then use a fork to fluff up the rice, and serve with the chicken masala.

CHEAT'S MINT RAITA

Real Indian chefs would come after you with a tandoor skewer if they caught you doing this. Meanwhile, this version is reasonably convincing, especially if you leave it in the fridge for 15 minutes before serving. Don't tell anyone.

SERVES 6
PREP TIME: NEGLIGIBLE

150g/5oz (small pot)
    plain yoghurt
1 small jar of ready made
    mint sauce (not jelly)

Gradually and thoroughly stir the mint sauce into the yoghurt until it looks and tastes right. Put in the fridge to rest for 15 minutes.

I'd love to big this up but that's all there is to it.

FRESH TOMATO CHUTNEY

If you are handy with a knife and a chopper upperer (see page 37), you can make this. If you want to pimp it, add 1 teaspoon of olive oil infused with black cardamom. Grind up the cardamom seeds in a pestle and mortar, and mix with the oil in a clean jar. Leave for at least a week before using. This obviously requires planning ahead.

SERVES 6
PREP TIME: 10 MINUTES

3 large tomatoes
1 small onion, peeled
    and finely diced
A handful of coriander
    (cilantro) leaves, chopped
Salt

Chop the tomatoes into quarters, scoop out the sloppy stuff in the middle and discard. You want the firm outer flesh for this. Thoroughly dice up what's left.

Mix everything together in a bowl, adding a tiny pinch of salt.

Leave to stand for 20 minutes at room temperature.

Serve with ready-made poppadoms. Making your own is like trying to make your own underpants. Shop ones are better.

COCONUT RED LENTIL DAHL

Dahl is based on lentils, which get a bad rap from a lot of food recidivists. But let's not kid ourselves: dahl has sustained hundreds of millions of people in India. It's the original street food, made in one pot and scooped up with chapatis (see page 86). Simple, nutritious, tasty.

SERVES 6
PREP TIME: 15 MINUTES
COOKING TIME: 35 MINUTES

200g/7oz/1 cup red
    split lentils
1 shallot, finely chopped
1 garlic clove, peeled
    and finely chopped
A small handful of dried
    curry leaves
1 small cinnamon stick
1 green chilli, finely chopped
    (deseeded, if preferred)
1 tsp hot curry powder
1 tsp salt
1 x 400ml/14fl oz can
    of coconut milk
Juice of ½ lemon
A small handful of coriander
    (cilantro) leaves, chopped,
    to garnish

Rinse the lentils in several changes of water until the water runs clear. This is important.

Put all the ingredients except the lemon juice and coriander leaves in a medium saucepan. Add 300ml/10fl oz/1¼ cups of water and bring to the boil.

Now reduce to a gentle simmer, stirring occasionally, for 30–35 minutes or until the lentils are soft. Add more water if you want it more soupy.

Season with the lemon juice and garnish with the coriander leaves.

Go forth and multiply.

CHAPATIS

I was amazed at how easy and convincing these were when I tried making them. These are proper restaurant-grade chapatis complete with browned craters where air bubbles had popped in the pan. Tear into strips and use as consumable cutlery on your curry night.

MAKES 10 CHAPATIS
PREP TIME: 15 MINUTES
COOKING TIME: 10 MINUTES

140g/5oz/scant 1 cup
    wholemeal flour
140g/5oz/scant 1 cup
    plain flour, plus a bit
    for dusting
1 tsp salt
1 tbsp sunflower oil
180ml/6fl oz/¾ cup
    hot water

**SHEEP-SHAPED
FLOUR HOOVER**

How it works There is a
small battery-operated
fan inside the body of
the beast. As you push it
around the floury worktop,
it sucks up leftover flour
through its 'mouth'.

For An ideal gift,
for someone else.

Against Less effective
even than a real sheep.

Destination 'That charity
shop box'.

In a large bowl, stir together the two flours and salt. Use a wooden spoon to stir in the oil and enough hot water to make a soft dough.

Knead the dough on a lightly floured surface for 5 minutes until it is smooth. Push away with the heels of your hands, turn through 90º, repeat, roll back up, repeat, for at least 5 minutes.

Divide into 10 pieces. Roll each piece into a ball and leave to rest for a few minutes.

On a lightly floured surface, use a floured rolling pin to flatten each ball until 5 mm/less than ¼ inch thick. Rotate as you roll and aim for roundness.

Heat a non-stick frying pan over a medium heat until it's smokin' hot. Don't add any oil.

Chuck in a chapati. Cook until the underside has brown spots (around 30 seconds). Flip and cook the other side.

Put on a plate in a warm oven. Keep going with the rest of the chapatis.

If cooking fails,
that smile guarantees
me a job as an insincere
local politician

LAMB KEEMA CURRY

This is a simple beginner's curry using off-the-shelf curry powder. One day, you may learn to make your own curry mixtures from scratch, but don't try it yet. You will starve to death.

SERVES 4
PREP TIME: 15 MINUTES
COOKING TIME: 50 MINUTES

3 tbsp vegetable oil
1 large onion, peeled
   and diced
2 garlic cloves, peeled
   and grated
4cm/1½ inch piece of
   ginger, peeled and grated
2 green chillies, chopped
500g/1lb 2oz minced
   (ground) lamb
2–3 tbsp medium
   curry powder
3 large tomatoes, diced small
2 tbsp plain yoghurt
200g/7oz frozen peas
1 small bunch of coriander
   (cilantro), leaves chopped

Heat the oil in a large frying pan and fry the onion until soft and golden – this should take up to 10 minutes, but don't allow the onion to burn.

Add the garlic, ginger and chillies the pan and cook for a further 5 minutes. The mixture should become most fragrant.

Add the lamb and fry until browned, stirring constantly. Break up any lumps.

Sprinkle the curry powder evenly over the mixture and stir for a minute or so. It will now smell so fantastic you will be faint with curry lust.

Bung in the tomatoes and bring to a simmer. Cook for a minute, then add the yoghurt, a pinch of salt and a good grind of black pepper. Cook on a gentle simmer for 30 minutes. If the curry starts to look dry, add a splash of water.

Add the frozen peas, cook for 5 minutes, then stir in the coriander.

Serve with basmati rice (see page 81), chapatis (see page 86), the fresh tomato chutney (see page 84) and more yoghurt, or even my fake raita (page 84).

Gary the cameraman, not looking like the sharpest tool in the kitchen

FAKE INDIAN RICE PUDDING

You'll be amazed at how exotic this tastes. We spent several centuries in Britain eating plain rice pudding, not realising that the magic of spices could transform it. This is almost a storecupboard saviour, except you probably don't keep saffron in your Cupboard of Plenty.

SERVES 4
PREP TIME: 10 MINUTES
COOKING TIME: 10 MINUTES

Seeds from 3 green
  cardamom pods
1 x 400g/14oz can of
  creamy rice pudding
Pinch of saffron strands
4 tbsp sultanas
3 tbsp chopped pistachios

Crush the cardamom seeds in your pestle and mortar (ahem).

Mix them and everything else except the pistachios with the rice pudding in a saucepan.

Heat gently, stirring, for 10 minutes or so. The rice pudding will turn slightly golden thanks to the saffron.

Allow to cool until tantalisingly warm but not hot.

Serve in ethnically interesting small bowls scattered with the chopped pistachios, along with a comment about how one of your friends found this recipe in her late grandmother's cookery book.

Rice pudding breaks free
of the Victorian workhouse

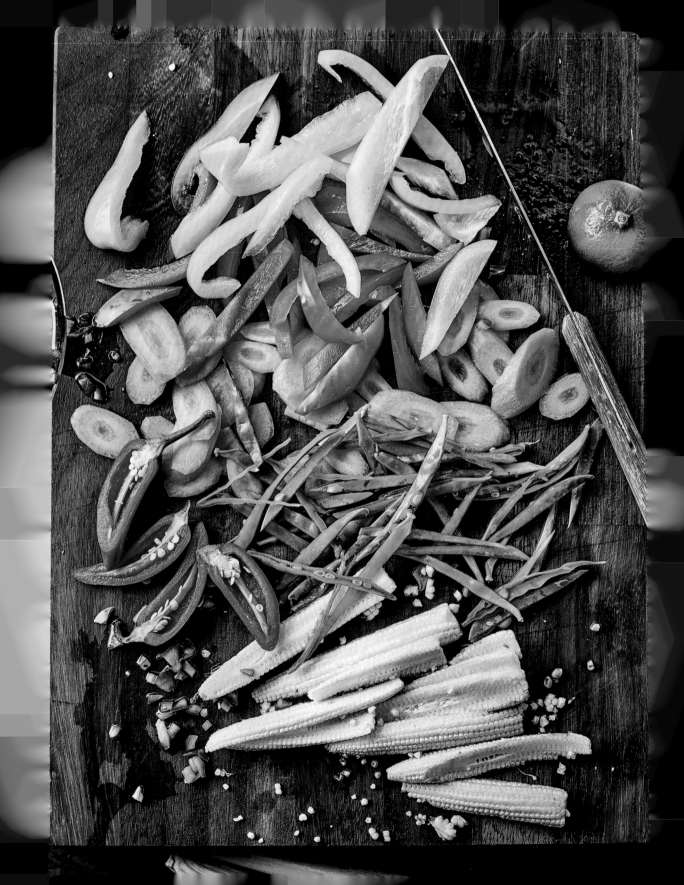

CHAPTER SIX
ASIAN FUSION

THAI CHICKEN NOODLE SOUP

During my childhood, chicken noodle soup came in a can as a clear chicken-inspired broth with some small pieces of plastic in the bottom. This Thai version is much better and includes lemongrass. Nothing bad ever came with lemongrass.

SERVES 4
PREP TIME: 20 MINUTES
COOKING TIME: 25 MINUTES

1 tbsp olive oil
450g/1lb boneless, skinless
  chicken breast, thinly sliced
2 garlic cloves, peeled and
  roughly chopped
1 tbsp Thai green curry paste
1 lemongrass stalk, finely sliced
1 tsp grated fresh ginger
1 litre/1¾ pints/4 cups
  hot chicken stock
75g/2½oz rice noodles
150g/5½oz mangetout
  (snow peas), halved
125g/4½oz bean sprouts
1 bunch of spring onions
  (scallions), sliced
2 tbsp Thai fish sauce
Grated zest and juice of 1 lime
A handful of fresh coriander
  (cilantro), chopped, to garnish

Heat the oil in a large pan over a medium heat. Add the chicken, garlic, curry paste, lemongrass and ginger, and cook, stirring, until the chicken is turning golden.

Add the hot stock and bring to the boil. Simmer gently for 5 minutes until the chicken is cooked through (if you're nervous, check by cutting a piece in half – there should be no pink meat).

Add the rice noodles and cook for 1 minute. Move them around to prevent them clumping together. Add the mangetout and cook for another 2 minutes.

Add the bean sprouts, spring onions, fish sauce, and the lime zest and juice. Simmer until heated through.

Divide the soup among four warmed bowls and garnish with the chopped coriander.

Swap stories about an amazing club you went to in Bangkok.

SPICY TOFU BROTH

Tofu, like celery, is of itself pointless, but makes a great bulking agent for a soup such as this one. It's also vegetarian. You could try the same recipe with any old veg or curd.

SERVES 4
PREP TIME: 10 MINUTES
COOKING TIME: 6–8 MINUTES

1 tbsp Thai red curry paste
200ml/7fl oz/scant 1 cup
  reduced-fat coconut milk
600ml/1 pint hot
  vegetable stock
200g/7oz tofu, cubed
2 pak choi, chopped
A handful of sugarsnap peas
4 spring onions (scallions), chopped

Heat the curry paste in a pan for a few minutes, then add the coconut milk and the stock and bring to the boil.

Bung in everything else. Reduce the heat and simmer (no lid) for a few minutes more.

Ladle into warm bowls and serve.

Immerse a spoon in the liquid and offer up to large hole in front of face.

JAMES'S TSUKUDANI
(STEWED SEAWEED)

I was shown how to make this in Japan. But, annoyingly, I didn't write it down, and so I've created this version from memory. I think it's roughly right but in any case it tastes terrific. I think you can store it in the fridge for quite a long time, but I always eat it all in one go, so I don't know.

SERVES 1
PREP TIME: 1 MINUTE
COOKING TIME: 30 MINUTES

5 nori seaweed sheets
250ml/9fl oz/1 cup plus
    1 tbsp water
2 tbsp cooking sake
1 tbsp dark soy sauce
1 tbsp toasted sesame oil
Some toasted sesame seeds

Crumble the seaweed sheets into a small pan and add the water. Let it stand for a few minutes until the seaweed has gone completely limp.

Bring to a gentle simmer, stirring to ensure the seaweed is entirely 'incorporated'. Beware of any seaweed sticking to the side of the pan.

Add the sake and continue simmering to reduce the mixture to a mash.

Add the soy sauce and sesame oil and simmer for a few more minutes.

Throw in the sesame seeds.

Decant into a clean jam jar and allow to cool.

Stir a spoonful into your Japanese breakfast rice bowl.

'Douitashimashite.' どういたしまして

Seaweed makes your hair go fuzzy

STIR-FRIED CHILLI BEEF

This will also work with shredded chicken or pork, but the beef version is the one approved by the Foreign Office. Add an extra chilli or two to turn this into 'dare food'. You'll spoil it, though.

SERVES 4
PREP TIME: 25 MINUTES +
HALF A DAY MARINATING TIME
COOKING TIME: 8 MINUTES (SIC)

1 tbsp sesame oil
1 tsp grated fresh ginger
2 tbsp soy sauce
1 green chilli, finely chopped
450g/1lb steak, cut into strips
1 red and 1 yellow (bell)
    pepper, deseeded and
    roughly chopped
1 carrot, cut into thin strips
250g/9oz baby corn
200g/7oz mangetout
    (snow peas), halved
300g/10½oz bean sprouts
300g/10½oz rice noodles
Sweet chilli sauce, to drizzle

In advance

Put the oil in a large bowl. Add the ginger, soy sauce, chilli and steak strips. Mix up and leave in the fridge, covered, to marinate for at least 10 minutes. Half a day is even better.

Later

Heat your wok (large frying pan if you haven't got one. Why haven't you got one?) until really hot. Remove the meat from the marinade and wipe dry. Reserve the marinade. Add the beef to the wok and stir fry for 5 minutes.

Now add the peppers, carrot, baby corn, mangetout, bean sprouts and the leftover marinade. Stir fry for 3 minutes until everything is cooked but not soggy.

At the same time, soak the noodles for 4 minutes (or however long the pack suggests), drain well and add to the pan. Toss well.

Serve straight away, anointed with chilli sauce.

SALMON & GINGER
WITH STIR-FRY VEG

You'll need to plan a few hours ahead to allow time for a good marinade, but then the next stage happens very quickly, especially the stir-fry, and especially if you use a proper, thin steel wok. It's worth investing a bit extra in a proper one. Relax your shoulders and arms to wield your wok like a true pro.

SERVES 2
PREP TIME: 10 MINUTES +
HALF A DAY MARINATING
COOKING TIME: 20 MINUTES

2 salmon fillets

For the marinade
3cm/1¼ inch piece of ginger, peeled and finely grated
1 garlic clove, peeled and finely grated
1 tbsp brown sugar
½ tbsp dark soy sauce
¼ tsp toasted sesame oil
Squeeze of ½ lime

For the stir-fry veg
½ tbsp vegetable oil
½ tbsp toasted sesame oil
1 garlic clove, peeled and thinly sliced
3cm/1¼ inch piece of ginger, peeled and cut into very thin matchsticks
1 red chilli, sliced
300g/10½oz mixed vegetables such as sugar snap peas, baby corn, red (bell) peppers, cut into strips, and 1 head of pak choi, cut into quarters
Dash of oyster sauce (cures everything)
1 tbsp light soy sauce

Combine all the marinade ingredients in a bowl and stir thoroughly until the sugar dissolves and you have a sticky mixture.

Put the salmon fillets pink side up on a plate and pour the marinade over the top. Leave in the fridge, covered, to marinate for a few hours. Half a day is even better if you have the time.

Alternatively, if you're in a hurry, crack on without waiting. It'll still taste pretty good.

Preheat the oven to 180ºC/350ºF.

Put the smothered fish on a lined baking sheet and bake for around 15 minutes, then take it out and leave to rest. In this small window you must complete the stir-fry.

Heat up the wok until it is blindingly hot.

Add the oils. Panic briefly, then quickly fry the garlic, ginger and chilli for 15 seconds or so.

Add all the vegetables except the pak choi and stir-fry flamboyantly for 2 minutes. (At this point you could add the dash of oyster sauce.)

Now add the pak choi, just long enough for it to go a bit limp.

Season with soy sauce and you're done.

This man is utterly underwhelmed
by his own achievements

↓

CHAPTER SEVEN

THE GREAT OUTDOORS

SPICY CHICKEN KEBABS

These are shish kebabs; that is, cooked on a skewer, and one of the greatest gifts that what we now call the Middle East bequeathed to the world. The best one I've ever had was in a marketplace in Damascus, a snack-sized offering cooked over real charcoal. I had five. Prepare these carefully and they'll be almost as good.

MAKES 4 KEBABS
PREP TIME: 10 MINUTES +
20 MINUTES' MARINATING TIME
COOKING TIME: 12–15 MINUTES

2 tbsp olive oil
A large handful of flat-leaf
     parsley, chopped
1 garlic clove, peeled
A good pinch of paprika
1 tsp ground cumin
Grated zest and juice of 1 lemon
4 boneless, skinless chicken
     breasts, cut into bite-
     sized chunks
1 red and 1 green (bell) pepper,
     deseeded and chopped
     into tantalising shapes

Prepare your barbecue. It is ready when it appears to have gone out: when the coals are grey, there are no flames, and it no longer smells of paraffin firelighter or diesel. Be patient.

While the barbecue is heating up, make the marinade. Put everything except the chicken and peppers into a food blender and whizz to a smooth paste.

Make small cuts on all sides of each piece of chicken to help with the marinading process. Arrange the chicken in a shallow dish and rub the paste well in.

Cover and leave in the fridge for at least 20 minutes.

While the chicken is marinating, soak four wooden skewers in cold water.

Thread the chicken pieces on to the skewers, alternating with red and green pieces of pepper.

Place on the hot barbecue. Turn the kebabs frequently, for 10–15 minutes, until the chicken is golden and the peppers slightly soft.

Consume. Stab the inside of your cheek with the end of the skewer, even though you told yourself you wouldn't.

STICKY BUFFALO WINGS

Buffalo wings do not come from buffalo, which have no wings, and if they did, they'd be bloody huge. Rather, they are so-called (it is believed) because the technique of marinating the chicken wings and then grilling was popular in Buffalo, New York State. This will serve six people at two wings each or four people at three wings each. You could probably have worked that out, though.

SERVES 4–6
PREP TIME: 10 MINUTES +
2 HOURS' MARINATING TIME
COOKING TIME: 20–30 MINUTES

4 tbsp runny honey
4 tbsp wholegrain mustard
2 tbsp dark soy sauce
12 chicken wings
Salt 'n' pepper

Mix the honey, mustard and soy sauce together in a large bowl, seasoning liberally.

Add the wings and turn to make sure they're evenly coated. Cover and leave in the fridge for 2 hours.

Prepare your barbecue. Remember that you are cooking chicken, not smelting iron. You want embers, not a chuffing fiery furnace that would look right to Abraham Darby. Be patient.

Remove the wings from the marinade and cook for at least 8 minutes on each side. Check the fattest part of the chicken to see if they are cooked through. The juices should run clear.

Now burn your face.

SPICY LIME PRAWNS

This could bring a little light and healthy Asian relief to the unrelenting and all-consuming bonfire that is your attempt at a barbecue. They will be thrown into stark, spicy relief by the piles of unwanted charred sausages and rock-hard 'baked' potatoes. Just make these.

SERVES 8
PREP TIME: 10 MINUTES + AT
LEAST 1 HOUR'S MARINATING TIME
COOKING TIME: 4 MINUTES

Grated zest and juice of 1 lime
1 garlic clove, peeled and crushed
2 small red chillies, deseeded
  and finely chopped
5 tbsp olive oil
32 peeled raw tiger prawns,
  defrosted if frozen
Pitta bread to serve

Put the lime zest and juice, garlic, chillies and oil in a screw-topped jar. Close the lid tightly and shake well.

Put the prawns in a shallow dish and add the lime marinade. Cover and marinate in the fridge for at least 1 hour.

Meanwhile, prepare your barbecue. You are not firing the boiler of Flying Scotsman; you are merely looking to produce an even layer of flame-free coals.

While the barbecue is heating up, soak eight bamboo skewers in cold water for 20 minutes.

Thread 4 prawns onto each skewer. Cook the skewers on the barbecue for 3–4 minutes on each side until they turn pink.

Serve immediately with warm pitta bread. You will have tried to warm it on the barbecue, so for 'warmed' read 'on fire'.

HOME-MADE CHEESEBURGERS

In the modern world, making your own burger patties is a bit like making your own self-assembly furniture kits – pointless. But it is satisfying, and you may be surprised how pure and simple a burger can taste if you've hitherto bought them from roadside caravans. You can also use vegetarian meat substitute, but add several tablespoons of vegetable oil to the mix, or you will be trying to eat the contents of an office shredder.

SERVES 6
PREP TIME: 1 HOUR 20
MINUTES, INCLUDING
CHILLING TIME
COOKING TIME: 12 MINUTES

1kg/2lb 4oz extra-lean minced
    (ground) beef
1 tbsp tomato ketchup
2 medium eggs, beaten
6 thin-cut slices of your
    chosen cheese
6 burger buns, halved
6 tbsp mayonnaise
6 lettuce leaves, shredded
3 large tomatoes,
    thickly sliced
6 cocktail gherkins, sliced
1 large onion, peeled and
    thinly sliced to make rings
Salt 'n' pepper

Put the beef, tomato ketchup and egg into a bowl. Season with a pinch of salt and a big grind of black pepper. Mix well together.

Divide into six equal portions and shape into balls. Now use the palm of your hand to flatten into patties. Make them uniformly thick for even cooking. They need to be roughly the diameter of your buns.

Put the patties on a tray and cover with clingfilm. Put them in the fridge for at least 1 hour. Chilling helps them bind together.

Prepare your barbecue. The coals should be grey and ashen, like a chemistry teacher's face, and there should be no flames. Be patient.

Add the patties to the hot grill. You should cook each one for between 5 and 6 minutes per side, depending on the thickness. Check the burger designated as your own with the point of a knife. It shouldn't be pink in the middle.

Don't be tempted to press the patties onto the griddle. This will squeeze out nourishing juices, which will drip onto the coals and create horrible smoke. Just leave them alone, for Pete's sake.

Once both sides are cooked, lay a slice of cheese on each patty and cook for another couple of minutes, until the cheese is half melted.

At the same time, lay your sliced buns inner-face down on the grill, to toast them lightly.

Now assemble the burger. Spread mayonnaise on the bottom half. Add the cheesy burger followed by the lettuce, the tomatoes, the gherkin and finally an onion ring. Add the lid.

Discover that the depth of the burger is greater than the maximum opening achievable with your mouth.

CHAR-GRILLED VEGETABLES

Vegetables are often overlooked at the barbecue, mainly because men assume control and turn what should be a cooking session into a pyromaniac carnivores' convention. These veg are easy to do and very tasty. If you overdo them, simply add them to the coals as a fuel supplement, and start again. This will happen automatically if you cut them up too small.

PREP TIME: 10 MINUTES +
2 HOURS' MARINATING TIME
COOKING TIME: 10–15 MINUTES

4 garlic cloves, peeled
   and crushed
6 tbsp olive oil
1 red and 1 yellow (bell) pepper,
   deseeded and cut into strips
2 courgettes (zucchini), sliced
1 aubergine (eggplant), cubed
1 sweet potato, peeled and
   cut into wedges
2 red onions, peeled and
   cut into wedges
Salt 'n' pepper

Add the garlic and olive oil to a clean screw-topped jam jar, stir well, close the lid and shake well. If you do this a few days beforehand the garlic flavour will be much greater.

Put the vegetables in a shallow dish and pour over the garlic oil. Add seasoning. Shake it all about to ensure everything is evenly coated. Cover and put in the fridge for at least 2 hours. If the vegetables aren't properly soaked in oil before cooking they will turn out dry and cardboardy.

Meanwhile, prepare your barbecue. If it is a charcoal type, remember that it takes a while to get going. Be patient.

Lay the vegetables in a single layer on the hot barbecue. Cook for 10–15 minutes, turning regularly. They are done when tender and starting to char. Discard and have a cheeseburger instead.

BROAD BEAN & FETA SALAD

There had to be a salad somewhere in this book, and here it is. It is offered here as an accompaniment to your barbecue, to lend it colour and an air of sophistication. But really you're manning a body parts' incinerator. Learn to squeeze the beans.

SERVES 4
PREP TIME: 10 MINUTES

450g/1lb broad (fava)
   beans, podded
175g/6oz feta cheese, diced
6 tbsp chopped fresh
   mint leaves
3 tbsp olive oil
Juice of 1 lemon
Salt 'n' pepper

Cook the beans in boiling water for around 6 minutes. Drain, douse with cold water (this keeps them looking green rather than grey) and leave to stand for a few minutes.

The skins should be slightly baggy, and if you squeeze one at the edge the bright green inner bean should pop out. Very satisfying. Actually, I like them with the skins on. Sarah likes them skin-off. We will forever be divided on this.

Put the beans in a bowl with everything else, season and mix together. Place ostentatiously on a table to be ignored.

CHAPTER EIGHT

SPONGEY THINGS

JAM ROLY POLY

The appeal of this classic pudding from the endless summer of childhood is not just its rich, dense flavour; it's also that 'roly poly' is a funny expression in the way 'spotted dick' isn't, actually. This is an easy version which is cooked in the oven rather than steamed on top. Convention specifies raspberry or strawberry jam, but it would probably work just as well with marmalade, Nutella, or thinly sliced Spam.

SERVES 4
PREP TIME: 20 MINUTES
COOKING TIME: 30–35 MINUTES

You will need a deep-sided roasting tin and a rack that fits inside it.

Softened butter, for greasing
200g/7oz/1⅓ cup self-raising (self-rising) flour, plus extra for dusting
100g/3½oz shredded beef (or vegetable) suet
1 tbsp caster sugar
Pinch of salt
150ml/5fl oz/⅔ cup semi-skimmed milk or water
6-7 tbsp raspberry or strawberry jam (jelly)

Preheat the oven to 200°C/400°F. Butter a large sheet of baking parchment and set aside.

Stir the flour, suet, sugar and salt in a large bowl until fully combined. Slowly stir in the milk or water to form a soft, spongey dough.

Tip the dough out onto a floured surface and knead for a few minutes. Roll the dough out into a 22 x 32cm/ 8½ x 13inch rectangle.

Spread the jam onto the dough, leaving a 1.5cm/½ in border around the edge. Slightly dampen the border with water. Gently roll the dough up from the short end and transfer to the baking parchment, seam-side down. Wrap the roly poly in the baking parchment, making a long pleat in the paper to allow the pudding to expand as it cooks. Twist the ends of the parchment like a Christmas cracker and tie tightly with kitchen string, to seal the pudding inside. Repeat the wrapping process with a large piece of kitchen foil.

Place the pudding on the roasting rack set inside the roasting tin. Pour boiling water halfway up the roasting tin, just to the base of the pudding, and cook in the oven for 30–35 minutes.

Remove the pudding from the oven, unwrap the kitchen foil, then snip the string and unwrap the parchment.

The pudding should be well risen and lightly browned in places. Don't worry if the jam has made its way through to the outside of the pudding and ends up on your face.

Place on a warmed serving plate and cut into thick slices. Serve with lots of My Perfect Custard (see page 119).

SPOTTED DICK

As hard as you might try, you will not be able to come up with an original or funny joke around the term 'spotted dick'. 'Dick', in this context, is an old English word meaning 'a steamed pudding'. Sometimes also known as 'spotted dog'. Still not funny.

SERVES 4
PREP TIME: 20 MINUTES
COOKING TIME: 1 1/2 HOURS

You will need baking parchment, foil, some string and a greased 1.2-litre/2-pint pudding basin, plus a tight-lidded saucepan large enough to sit the basin in.

Softened butter, for greasing
300g/10½oz/2 cups flour
2 tsp baking powder
150g/5½oz shredded beef
   (or vegetable) suet
85g/3oz/⅓ cup caster sugar
125g/4½oz/¾ cup currants
Zest of 1 lemon
200ml/7fl oz/scant 1 cup milk

Butter the inside of the pudding basin.

Throw everything except the milk into a large bowl and mix to combine thoroughly.

Now add the milk gradually and stir to make a soft dough. There should be no lumps or puddles.

Spoon the mixture into the pudding basin.

You now have to make a hat for the basin from baking parchment and foil. Tear off a piece of each larger than the top of the bowl. Place the foil on top of the paper and make a generous pleat across the middle, like the one in your history teacher's trousers. This allows the covering to expand as the pudding steams.

Tie this paper and foil top securely around the rim of the bowl with string. The pleat should span the middle.

Place a small plate or saucer into the bottom of the saucepan (it prevents the bottom of the pudding bowl becoming too hot), then sit the basin on top. Fill the pan two-thirds with water.

Put the lid on the pan, bring to the boil and simmer for 1½ hours. Check the water level periodically. It mustn't run dry. Top it up with more boiling water if necessary.

Let the pudding sit for 15 minutes before unwrapping and tipping out onto a warmed serving plate.

Serve with My Perfect Custard, see opposite.

Continue your attempts at a 'dick' joke.

MY PERFECT CUSTARD

Ready-made or instant custard is hard to beat, and you should have some to hand in your storecupboard in case you cock this up. But you will earn tons of kudos for making your own. This is enough for six people, leaving you some left over to have with sliced bananas, or as a soup for breakfast.

SERVES 6
PREP TIME: 5 MINUTES
COOKING TIME: 20 MINUTES

568ml/1 pint/2½ cups
    full fat (whole)milk
1 vanilla pod, slit in half
    lengthways and seeds
    scraped out
6 egg yolks
2 tbsp caster sugar
1 tbsp cornflour

VOMITING CHICKEN

How it works The whole egg is cracked into the chicken's head. Tip it up, and only the white comes out of its mouth, making for easy separation.

For Sort of works, cute.

Against Can choke on its own vomit.

Destination Kitchen window sill.

Put the milk into a thick-bottomed pan with the vanilla pod and seeds. Heat gently, stir and bring to just below a simmer. Do not allow it to boil.

Meanwhile, beat the egg yolks, sugar and cornflour together in a large bowl.

Fish the vanilla pod out of the hot milk and bin it. Leave in the seeds. Pour the milk into the yolk and sugar mixture, stirring all the time.

Turn the heat down as low as it will go and pour the custard back into the pan. Stir slowly and continuously. The custard is done when it just coats the back of a wooden spoon. Cook longer for a thicker version.

Decant into a warmed jug. Serve immediately.

Hide the instant custard tin, or no one will believe you made this.

WHAT TO DO WITH 6 EGG WHITES?
It would be immoral, in this day and age, to waste these. You could always:

Make a fashionable egg-white omelette, as favoured by slimming nazis, but it's a very unsatisfying experience.

Make a meringue, but it's a bit of a faff to be honest, and it sticks in your teeth.

Mix with with water and spread the mixture evenly over your face. Leave for 10 minutes and then rinse off. You should observe reduced puffiness and tighter pores. Or egg on face.

VICTORIA SPONGE

There is a story concerning the relationship between this spongey wonder and our po-faced eponymous monarch, but it's far too dreary for a book like this. The queen is dead. Long live the cake.

MAKES 1 CAKE
PREP TIME: 30 MINUTES
COOKING TIME: 25 MINUTES
+ COOLING TIME

You will need two 18-cm/
  7-inch sandwich tins.

3 big eggs – weigh them
  together in their shells
  and note the weight
  (this is important)
The same weight of each
  of: softened butter (plus
  a bit extra to grease),
  caster sugar and self-raising
  (self-rising) flour, sifted
1 tsp baking powder
1–2 tbsp milk
6 tbsp raspberry jam (jelly)
250ml/9fl oz/1 cup
  double (heavy) cream,
  whipped until stiff
Icing (confectioners') sugar,
  for dusting

Preheat the oven to 180ºC/350ºF.

Lightly grease the sandwich tins with butter and line the bases with baking parchment.

In a large bowl, beat the butter and caster sugar together until pale and fluffy.

Now beat in the eggs, one at a time, with a spoonful of flour. Mix together well. Fold in the remaining flour and baking powder with a large metal spoon. Add 1–2 tablespoons of milk. The batter should just drop off the spoon but without being runny.

Divide the mixture equally between the prepared tins and shake down to level the surface.

Bake in the centre of the oven for 20–25 minutes until the sponges are well risen and golden on top. They should spring back if you press them gently in the middle.

Remove from the oven but leave to cool in the tins for 5 minutes.

Run a knife around the edges of the cakes and turn out. Remove the lining paper (*important!*) and leave them to cool base side down on a wire rack. These bases will become the middle of the cake.

When cool, layer one half with the jam, and the other with the whipped cream.

In one confident and fearless move, invert one half onto the other. Dust the surface of the cake with sifted icing sugar.

Cut into vulgar segments and shove in face.

*May the sun never set
on Victoria's sponge*

CHAPTER NINE

STORE-CUPBOARD SAVIOURS

STORECUPBOARD SAVIOURS

In one corner of the May household's kitchen is what I call The Cupboard of Plenty. This is where I keep all the things that would sustain me if the zombies came; things that never go off, and that can be transformed into dazzling Armageddon cuisine in a trice. The oldest item in there is a canned steak 'n' kidney pudding with a use-by date of 1998. Here's what could be in yours.

Dried things
Various pastas
Noodles
Pot noodles
Rice
Dried fruit pieces
Dried mushrooms
Miso soup sachets
Seaweed
Lentils

Canned things
Spam
Tomatoes
Mixed beans
Kidney beans
Baked beans
Baked beans and sausages
Spam
Sardines, mackerel, anchovies
Spaghetti hoops
Hot-dog sausages
Hearty soups
Spam
Coconut milk
Rice pudding
Custard
Spam

Sauces
Tomato
Brown
Soy
Worcestershire
Teriyaki
Salad cream
Lime pickle
Mango chutney

Essential spices
Salt
Black peppercorns
Various ready-made
   curry powders
Thai green curry paste
Nasi goreng sachet
Ground ginger
Whole cumin seeds
Whole fennel seeds
Brown cardamom pods
Star anise
Chinese five-spice
Dried chilli flakes
Paprika
Wasabi in a tube

Nuclear winter miscellany
Packet of mixed fruit and nut
Jar of gherkins
Pickled onions
Pickled eggs
Packet of ready-grated Parmesan
Unidentifiable packet snacks
   from the Asian supermarket
Spare can of Spam

MINESTRONE
WITH CRAP CROÛTONS

'Life is a minestrone,' sang 10cc back in 1975, but they were wrong. Minestrone is, in fact, a soup. Its exact composition is a subject of great debate, but rather than becoming embroiled in that, I've devised a hearty interpretation with beans and pasta, for winter warmth. It comes with quick-fix croûtons, made from toast. No-one will be fooled.

SERVES 4
PREP TIME: 10 MINUTES
COOKING TIME: 45 MINUTES

2 tbsp olive oil
1 onion, peeled and
    finely chopped
2 carrots, peeled
    and chopped
1 celery stick, chopped
2 garlic cloves, peeled
    and crushed
A few sprigs of fresh thyme
1 litre/1¾ pints hot
    vegetable stock
1 x 400g/14oz can of
    chopped tomatoes
1 x 400g/14oz can of
    borlotti or cannellini
    beans, drained
125g/4½oz soup pasta or
    other bits of leftover pasta
    shapes, broken up
2 slices of any old bread
Salt 'n' pepper

Heat the oil in a large saucepan and add the onion, carrots and celery. Cook over a low heat for 10 minutes until soft.

Add the garlic and thyme and cook for another 2–3 minutes.

Add the hot stock, tomatoes and beans. Bring to the boil, then reduce and simmer for around 20 minutes.

Add the soup pasta (or other leftover bits of pasta broken up) and cook for another 10 minutes, until the vegetables are tender and the pasta is cooked.

Now remove the thyme and taste. Add seasoning to taste.

While the soup is cooking, toast the slices of bread quite well, so they're crispy. Cut them into small squares.

Ladle the soup into warmed bowls and add the croûtons just before serving.

PIMPED-UP
ALPHABET PASTA ON TOAST

Pesto, even from a jar, is considered quite highbrow. Alphabet spaghetti from a can is only marginally less contemptible than chicken dippers. But bring them together...

SERVES: 4
PREP TIME: 1 MINUTE
COOKING TIME: 10 MINUTES

1 x 400g/14oz can of
    alphabet spaghetti
    in tomato sauce
4 slices of white bread
1 small jar of pesto
4 tbsp grated Parmesan
    cheese (from a packet)

Heat up the pasta in a small saucepan, without letting it boil.

Toast the bread, and spread the slices generously with pesto.

Top with the pasta and finish off with the grated cheese.

Bollocks to the River Café.

CHILLI CHEESE ON TOAST

This is simple cheese on toast with a bit of a kick, courtesy of the chillies. Heat lightens the stodginess of the melted cheese and will quickly bring you round from a thick head.

SERVES 4
PREP TIME: 10 MINUTES
COOKING TIME: 5 MINUTES

4 slices of white bread
100g/3½oz mature
    Cheddar, grated (ideally
    in the Mouli grater)
1 green chilli, deseeded
    and finely chopped
¼ tsp dried chilli flakes
2 spring onions (scallions),
    thinly sliced
Knobs of butter, for
    spreading (optional)

Preheat the grill to high – if electric, it should be glowing red.

Put the bread in the toaster and toast to taste.

Meanwhile, mix the cheese, chillies and spring onions together in a bowl.

Butter the toast, if you like, and then pile the cheesy mix on top, spreading evenly and right to the edges.

Put the slices under the grill.

They are ready when the cheese is bubbling and turning golden.

You are impatient, so you will burn your mouth.

SARDINES ON TOAST

Someone once said there is no poverty between the sheets. There's no poverty on toast, either. Sardines on toast combines two of the world's greatest cheap luxuries: sardines and toast.

SERVES 1
PREP TIME: 10 MINUTES
COOKING TIME: 5 MINUTES

1 small gherkin from a jar
1 x 95g/3½oz can of sardines
   in sunflower or olive oil
1 heaped tbsp salad cream
2 slices of white bread
Knob of butter, for
   spreading (optional)
Black pepper
A few token sprigs of fresh
   parsley, to garnish

Preheat the grill to high – if electric, it should be glowing red.

Slice the gherkin across into wafer-thin pieces.

Decant the sardines into a bowl, keeping all the oil.

Add the salad cream, a generous twist of black pepper and the sliced gherkin.

Start the bread in the toaster now.

Mash up everything in the bowl until it's a consistent coarse paste, with no recognisable sections of sardine visible.

Butter the toast, if you like. Spread the sardine mixture evenly on the buttered side right up to the edges.

Whack under the grill until the surface of the sardine mix bubbles gently and begins to form a crust.

Cut into elegant triangles and garnish each one with a tiny sprig of parsley, for appearances.

Discard the parsley and eat.

MINGING HOT DOGS

The hot dog, unlike the cheeseburger, has largely resisted gentrification.
These are so terrible (yet strangely delicious) that trying to produce a 'gourmet'
version is laughable. For the authentic experience, use the cheapest and most
basic industrial ingredients you can find. These can never be good for you,
so let's make them really baaaaaad.

ALLOW 2 ROLLS PER PERSON
PREP TIME: 5 MINUTES
COOKING TIME: 10 MINUTES

1 tbsp vegetable oil
1 onion, peeled and sliced
   but not too finely
1 can or packet of hot-dog
   sausages – wieners
   or frankfurters
1 pack of blow-away-austerity
   white bread rolls
English mustard and
   tomato ketchup from
   squeezy bottles

Add the oil to a frying pan and cook the onion over a medium heat until the onion is just starting to turn brown. Don't let the slices burn.

Meanwhile, there are three ways to cook the 'sausages'.

Steam
Arrange the sausages in a large, lidded frying pan. Add hot water to about half the thickness of the snorkers. Bring to the boil, put the lid on and leave for around 8 minutes. Check the pan doesn't boil dry. Add more boiling water if necessary. This is the 'proper' way.

Grill
Arrange the sausages on a grill pan. Put under a medium–high heat and turn regularly for 10 minutes. Then turn the heat up to 11 and give them a blast all round to brown the outsides.

BBQ
Place the sausages in a mesh basket, place on the hot barbecue and turn regularly to create griddle marks, until the sausages are blackened on the outside but still stone cold in the middle. The advantage of this method is that the vile taste of the sausages will be disguised by that of the paraffin firelighters.

When the sausages are ready, slit the bread rolls lengthways, but not quite all the way through. Add a sausage. Garnish with the fried onions and then finish off with one wavy line each of mustard and ketchup.

Repeat until old people tell you how they had one like this when they went to see *Towering Inferno* in 1974.

ROAST BLOCK OF SPAM

There have been countless attempts to drag Spam into the realm of 'cuisine', such as Spam bourguignon and Spam au vin, but why bother? It's intended as a complete and self-contained foodstuff. Here is a simple recipe involving a glaze, which can be omitted. It tastes like your grandparents' anecdotes.

SERVES 4
PREP TIME: 5 MINUTES
COOKING TIME: 30 MINUTES

1 tbsp wine vinegar (optional)
½ tsp mustard powder (optional)
¼ tsp fennel seeds, crushed (optional)
A pinch of brown sugar (optional)
1 x 200g/7oz can of Spam

Preheat the oven to 190ºC/375ºF.

In a teacup, stir together the vinegar, mustard powder, fennel seeds and sugar.

Remove the Spam from the can in a single piece, using your preferred method. Roughly score all the surfaces with the tines of a fork.

Place the Spam on a metal baking sheet. Give the glaze a final stir and drizzle it over the top. Make sure plenty of it sticks to the sides (use a pastry brush to help you).

Bake in the oven for 15 minutes. Then turn the block over, baste with the glaze and bake for another 15 minutes.

Remove from the oven and cut into slices. Serve with fried eggs (see page 26).

SPAMEN
(SPAM RAMEN)

Pot noodles, despite their reputation among food snobs, can be excellent. Look for the proper stuff from Japan, Korea or Thailand. This recipe is really pimped pot noodles, with my deepest apologies to any Japanese readers. Be careful frying the Spam. The first time I tried it, I burned the cornflakes, and not many people have said that.

SERVES 1
PREP TIME: 15 MINUTES
COOKING TIME: 6 MINUTES

3 fingers of Spam (eat the rest in a sandwich)
2 tbsp flour
2 eggs, beaten
1 cup cornflakes, finely crushed
Sunflower oil, for frying
1 pot noodle of your choice
A few pak choi leaves
1 egg, medium-boiled and cut in half
1 red chilli, finely sliced
1 spring onion (scallion), finely sliced
Chilli oil, to serve

Dip the Spam in the flour, then in the egg, then roll it in the cornflakes to coat. Dip in the egg and the cornflakes again, pressing them into the Spam. This makes a right mess.

In a deep frying pan heat a couple of centimetres of oil until really hot. Place the Spam in the oil, swearing profusely. Cook for a couple of minutes and then turn over. The fingers should be golden brown all over. The Spam fingers, not yours.

Remove from the oil and drain on kitchen roll.

Meanwhile, make the pot noodle according to the instructions and let it stand.

Blanch the pak choi in boiling water, cool briefly under cold water, then drain.

Decant the noodles, with a stir, into an exquisite Japanese red lacquered bowl. Arrange the pak choi to one side and the sliced egg to the other.

Top with the Spam and sprinkle with the chilli and spring onion. Finish with a drizzle of chilli oil.

APPLE CRUMBLE

Canned fruit (in juice not syrup) is full of goodness and lasts a very long time. That's why it's given to armies in the field. If you have some in your Cupboard of Plenty, with a bit of imagination it can be turned into this delicious crumble. No one will know it started life as a forgotten can. I used apple because that's what I had in my cupboard. You can make this with other fruit such as pears, peaches, apricots or even mixed fruit, or tomatoes.

SERVES 4
PREP TIME: 20 MINUTES
COOKING TIME: 30 MINUTES

2 x 400g/14oz cans of apple slices, drained of any juice
100g/3½oz/¾ cup flour
70g/2½oz/⅓ cup cold butter, diced into small cubes
70g/2½oz/¾ cup rolled oats
100g/3½oz demerara (raw brown) sugar

Preheat the oven to 200°C/400°F.

Place the apple slices in a shallow ovenproof dish.

In a large bowl, rub the flour and butter together between your fingertips until the mixture resembles breadcrumbs. Use a sort of combined squeezing and tossing action, like a mystic.

Mix in 50g/1¾oz of the oats and 70g/2½oz of the sugar.

Sprinkle the apples with this mixture and top with the remaining oats and sugar.

Bake in the oven for about 30 minutes or until it is golden brown and crisp on top.

Enjoy with ready-made tinned custard or you could use custard powder. Obviously. (Or better still, use My Perfect Custard recipe page 119.)

INCONSEQUENTIAL TRIFLE

Trifle, like Christmas, is not meant to be sophisticated or tasteful. It's supposed to be gaudy and plebeian. This one is made entirely from hospital ingredients and will taste as good as any.

SERVES 4
PREP TIME: 10 MINUTES

Biscuits of your choice
  (I used oaty Hobnobs),
  crumbed (reserve 1 biscuit
  for the garnish)
1 x 400g/14oz can of fruit
  cocktail in juice
2 tubs of ready-made jelly
  (Jello dessert)
1 x 400g/14oz can of custard
Squirty cream
Glacé cherries, to decorate

In four truly gopping retro beakers or goblets, first put in a layer of crushed biscuit.

Add a layer of fruit, followed by a layer of jelly, and then a layer of custard. You could add a dash of whisky to the fruit layer if feeling festive.

Top with a swirl of squirty cream, working from the wrist to create a 'Mister Whippy' effect. Crumble the remaining biscuit and sprinkle over the top of the cream. Balance a cherry on top.

Serve to gales of derision.

INDEX

ACKNOWLEDGEMENTS

This book, and the accompanying TV series, would not have been possible
without the help of quite a few people, starting with my mum, who showed
me how to make a cheese sauce when I was a teenager.

They also include everyone at Pavilion, otherwise publishers of proper
cookery books, for suppressing their horror when on set, and everyone at
Plum Pictures and New Entity, for their patience and forbearing during filming.

Thanks are also due to the UK Government for instigating the COVID-19
lockdown just as the deadline for this book approached, because if
I hadn't been forced to stay at home I'd never have finished it.

Finally, I would like to thank my agent, Fiona, because that's what you do in TV.